KU-337-245

the truth

ARMY FOUNDATION COLLEGE HARROGATE	
107770	
	11.05.07
155.9042	£4.99

OXFORD
UNIVERSITY PRESS

Great Clarendon Street, Oxford OX2 6DP

Oxford University Press is a department of the University of Oxford.
It furthers the University's objective of excellence in research, scholarship,
and education by publishing worldwide in

Oxford   New York

Auckland   Cape Town   Dar es Salaam   Hong Kong   Karachi
Kuala Lumpur   Madrid   Melbourne   Mexico City   Nairobi
New Delhi   Shanghai   Taipei   Toronto

With offices in

Argentina   Austria   Brazil   Chile   Czech Republic   France   Greece
Guatemala   Hungary   Italy   Japan   Poland   Portugal   Singapore
South Korea   Switzerland   Thailand   Turkey   Ukraine   Vietnam

Oxford is a registered trade mark of Oxford University Press
in the UK and in certain other countries

Text copyright © Ann McPherson and Aidan Macfarlane 2005
Illustrations by Tim Kahane 2005

The moral rights of the authors have been asserted

Database right Oxford University Press (maker)

First published 2005

All rights reserved. No part of this publication may be reproduced,
stored in a retrieval system, or transmitted, in any form or by any means,
without the prior permission in writing of Oxford University Press,
or as expressly permitted by law, or under terms agreed with the appropriate
reprographics rights organization. Enquiries concerning reproduction
outside the scope of the above should be sent to the Rights Department,
Oxford University Press, at the address above

You must not circulate this book in any other binding or cover
and you must impose this same condition on any acquirer

British Library Cataloguing in Publication Data
Data available

ISBN-13: 978-0-19-911311-8

ISBN-10: 0-19-911311-4

1 3 5 7 9 10 8 6 4 2

Printed in Great Britain
by Cox & Wyman Ltd., Reading, Berkshire

Third-party website addresses referred to in this publication are
provided by Oxford University Press in good faith and for information only.
Oxford University Press disclaims any responsibility for the material
contained therein.

Contents

AFC LIBRARY

All about stress

Our lives are full of changes and stress. They often go together. Stress is what we may feel as we try to adapt or cope with changes – changes at school, family changes, work changes, physical changes like puberty, relationship changes, and more.

On the good side, a bit of stress gives us the buzz to cope with these changes. The changes that happen inside us from having to cope with changes outside can make us more aware of life and help us feel more confident about dealing with the future. So the right amount of stress can be good for us. It can add to our excitement about life and make us feel stronger.

But too much stress and you may feel overwhelmed. You can't think straight – your thoughts begin to just run and run. You feel jumpy and nervous because you just have so much to do. Everyone and everything starts to get to you – your family, your friends, your teachers. You begin to have trouble doing your schoolwork because there is so much of it, and it's so, so difficult. You are tired all the time, moody, scratchy, snappy, anxious about everything – all because you're...

SOOOO STRESSSSSSSSSSSSSSSSSSSSSSSSSSSSSSSED.

Life, friends, relationships, work can all, at one time or another, go 'over the top' and bring on feelings of total helplessness. It may make us want to run away, cry, and feel as if we just can't go on.

How well you deal with stress will depend on how 'strong' you are feeling about the rest of your life. One thing for certain is that when you are tired, feeling run down or feeling ill, you won't be so good at dealing with stress. In fact, you can feel more ill when you are stressed and you can get more stressed when you are ill – your mind and your body interact with one another.

There is a certain amount of stress which is right for you but maybe not for someone else, a certain amount which is right for you at one time but maybe not at another. You don't want to cut stress out of your life completely, but you do need to learn how to cope with it. Not enough stress and you can get bored and depressed; too much and you get anxious and overwhelmed.

Some 'over the top' stressed people look for a quick fix. They try alcohol, drugs, cutting, shouting – all of which may help for a very short time but don't deal with the basic problems causing the stress. These quick fixes just help to blot out the real world for a bit, but the real world is still there when the effects wear off and they may leave you with even more problems.

Dealing with stress is about NOT hitting your head against the wall. It is about learning ways to deal with it. It is about being patient and believing that you can cope. It is about nibbling away at each problem, a bit at a time, so that you don't feel overwhelmed. It is about taking control again. It is about giving yourself some space. It is about deciding what you do need to deal with and what you don't.

- **READ THE EMAILS HERE AND SEE WHAT HAPPENS TO OTHER PEOPLE**

- **READ THE EMAILS HERE AND SEE HOW OTHER PEOPLE HAVE LEARNT TO DEAL WITH IT**

- **READ THE EMAILS HERE AND GET THE VERY BEST IDEAS ABOUT WHAT IS GOING TO HELP YOU**

What are the causes of stress

Our everyday lives are sometimes totally free of irritations and stresses and we feel fine. At other times our whole lives seem overwhelmed by annoyances and people being horrid to us. But we have to learn to take the rough with the smooth, and part of doing that is learning how not to get overwhelmed by it all. Here, and in the next chapter, are the range of things that have caused other teenagers to be stressed at one time or another. These problems are dealt with in greater detail in the following chapters.

● THERE MAY BE NO OBVIOUS REASON

Dear Doctor Ann, **I feel angry all the time for no reason.** 12 year old girl.

> *Dear 'Feeling angry'* – It may be that you are right that there is no reason for you feeling angry, but it may also be that you just cannot identify what the reason is yet. Young people often

have mood changes around the time of puberty and can't pinpoint what it is all about. Keep a diary of your angry feelings to see if they do relate to periods or anything else going on in your life. Also, it might help to make a list of the things that make you happy

and the things that make you angry to see if you can get any clues. Making sure you do regular exercise may also help get rid of some of those angry feelings.

Dear Doctor **Why are girls under pressure more than boys?** Girl aged 11.

Dear 'Why are girls under more pressure than boys?' – I am not sure that this is true. Girls and boys are under equal pressure, but girls may react more strongly to some of these pressures. Almost all boys and almost all girls – and almost all adults – feel pressure at one time or another. It may be over work, it may be over money, it may be over relationships, but the fact is that we all have to learn to cope with stress some way or other. We do know a bit about the difference between boys and girls in their early teens when it comes to what they worry about and therefore what stresses them, though...

- **School**   **boys 25%**   **girls 38%**
- Money   boys 23%   girls 32%
- **Health**   **boys 15%**   **girls 24%**
- Looks   boys 27%   girls 54%
- **HIV/Aids**   **boys 12%**   **girls 13%**
- Smoking   boys 12%   girls 16%
- **Drinking**   **boys 9%**   **girls 19%**

Real stress comes from just having too many problems to deal with at one time, and feeling overwhelmed by them all. So the best thing to do is 'bite off' a bit of each problem, one at a time, and don't try to face up to all of them at the same time – whether you are a boy or a girl!

• IT IS NOT ALWAYS THE BIG THINGS

Dear Dr. Ann, **I get so stressed all the time! Most of the time it's just about little things like not getting my own way. I constantly feel like I'm slipping into depression. I feel so alone and that I have no one to talk to. I always feel so useless. Please help.**
P.S. I feel that taking up a sport always helps me to relieve stress. I took up trampolining a few years ago and now I compete internationally! Girl aged 13.

Dear 'Stressed out by little things' – Not getting your own way can be stressful, but it is not good to get your own way all the time. So only get stressed about it when it stops you doing something that really, really matters to you. Your PS is very important, though – exercise can help stress, and it doesn't matter very much what the exercise is, as long as you enjoy it. As for feeling you are slipping into depression: stress and depression do sometimes go together, but not always. Stress itself can make you feel lonely and useless. We nearly all have these feelings from time to time. Talking to your parents might help, and sometimes all that is needed is reassurance that you are doing OK. Competing in international trampolining must have its own stresses, but it certainly means that you are not useless, even if you feel like it now and then.

Dear Dr. Ann, **just about everything really stresses me out!** 12 year old boy.

Dear 'Stressed by everything' – Perhaps it only feels like everything is stressing you out and you are only remembering the times you feel stressed and forgetting the times you feel OK. That's not to say that when you do feel stressed, it doesn't feel horrible. For a few days, write down all the things that are stressing you and all the things – and I am sure there will be some – that you can do without feeling stressed. Then read chapters 9 and 10 of this book, which deal with the ways others cope with stress and give some of my own tips on how to cope with it.

HAVING TOO MUCH TO COPE WITH

Dear doc, **If you are stressed sometimes it could be because you are taking on a lot of work at school or even extra stuff outside of school.** 15 year old girl.

Dear 'If you are stressed' – You are so right, but it may be that you *have* to do extra work inside or outside school. This is, as you say, the cause of stress. It's a time when you are pretty stretched anyway, and then there is more stuff that you have to do because life or work demands it. It could be that you have loads of routine schoolwork to do and you also have to revise for an exam. Or you may be having to do a paper round in the early morning because you need the extra money just to do things like buy clothes to go to school in. Or maybe you are caring for your mum or dad at home because they aren't well, and some of their care falls on you. The most stressful things in life are often things which you just have to do and can't get out of doing, even if they do cause you stress.

Dear Doctor Ann, **I got pregnant at 14 and now have a little boy but I need some advise on how to look after him as I get stressed.** 15 year old girl.

Dear '15 year old with a baby boy and stress' – I'm not surprised that you need some advise on how best to look after your son. It's very difficult suddenly finding yourself in this position at any age, but especially when you are 15 and most of your friends are out enjoying themselves, which probably means that you are a bit lonely. Everyone who has a baby should be in touch with a health visitor, who works with your family doctor. These are nurses specially trained to help people who have babies and young children, so please do feel you can ask her for help and confide in her. She may run special 'get togethers' for younger girls with babies. She should also be able to give you lots of books, including one about children aged 0–5, leaflets and videos, and to help make sure you get all the benefits and education that is available. I am not sure whether you are living at home or are in touch with your mum – if so, do ask her to help. Make sure that you are getting all the money benefits and other help that you are entitled to, and do continue your school education.

Ann, **what should you do when you are really annoyed with your family or friend/boyfriend!!!!!!!!!!** 14 year old girl.

Dear 'What to do when annoyed with family or friend' – You might need a reality check here by first asking yourself what your friends and family might find annoying about you. The reason for doing this is that it might give you some ideas about how to handle things that you find annoying about them. We all find people – even our nearest and dearest – annoying at one time or another, and they sometimes find us annoying in just the same way. We all have to learn to be a bit tolerant of other people's behaviour and hope that the things that we find annoying about them are outweighed by the good things about them. So the first thing to do when you are getting annoyed is to be patient and count up to 10 before doing anything else. The second thing to do is discuss with them what you find annoying. To do this in a non-threatening way, you can start by asking, 'You must find some things that I do very annoying, so please can we talk about them?' Then, when you have discussed these, you can say, 'And by the way, can we discuss one or two things that I find annoying about the way that you...' and so on. This should work both with your family and with your friends!

Dear Doctor Ann, **I'm 15 and have no friends and it stresses me out. What should I do!** 14 year old girl.

Dear 'I have no friends' – Friends can be very, very helpful when it comes to stopping you from getting stressed. They can be good to talk to, and good for helping you out when you have too many things to do or need help with schoolwork, etc. Of course they can also, just occasionally, be the cause of stress as well, because you care about your friends and what they do. Making friends, though, is not always easy and needs a bit of practice. The problem is that if one is desperate to make friends, then other people sense this and tend to back off. So you need to be pretty cool about it all and just put yourself in situations where you meet lots of people. You can begin by just trying to start a very simple conversation about something you saw on TV last night and liked. You always need to remember that many other people also find making friends difficult, so if you are willing to break the ice by making the first move in a conversation, the other person may be very responsive and keep things going. Sometimes it helps to join

some sort of activity club like drama, sport or music – then friendships develop because you have a common interest. Anyhow, the main thing is to have a try.

● SCHOOL AND EXAMS

Hey Ann, **I get soooo stressed with most things. I hate school at the minute cos I'm sooo unhappy and stressed with everything. Now I'm starting my GCSEs it's just getting worse!** I HATE MY LIFE!! Help!! 14 year old girl.

Dear 'Sooo stressed with most things' – I think that there are very few people who are not stressed when taking GCSEs – and they are either very, very lucky or very, very slack! With the underlying stresses of GCSE hanging over you, it is going to mean that you find everything else that adds to that stress particularly annoying and difficult. If you are willing to work really hard revising for your GCSEs, then I think that you should be let off doing other chores. Why not talk to your

parents and your teacher about the way you feel, and ask if you can be allowed to just get on with your GCSE work and not be asked to do anything else like the washing-up or shopping or whatever? But do allow yourself some breaks from just book work, and try to get some exercise as well, as that helps.

● IT CAN BE THINGS THAT OTHERS DO

Dear Doctor Ann, **I get really stressed when I see anyone smoking or selling drugs or drunk.** 11 year old girl.

Dear 'Getting stressed with people who smoke, take drugs or get drunk' – Yup, you have something in common with a large number of other people. Part of the stress comes from knowing that these people are harming themselves or other people, and that seems a really stupid thing to do. Another part of the stress comes from some of the people who take drugs or who are drunk being out of control, and they may therefore appear to be quite threatening. You may also be worried that they might try to pressurize you into trying these things too. The good news is that, although most young people will, at one time or another, experiment with smoking, drugs and drinking, most of them find that they don't want to go on 'doing' them, and give them up fairly soon.

Dear Doctor Ann, **I get stressed because of bullying – how do I counter it.** 13 year old boy.

Dear 'Getting stressed because of bullying' – I am so sorry that this is happening to you. I get a great many emails from young people who are bullied, and this is some of their advice on how to counter it...

'When I was bullied I just ignored what everyone said, no matter how hard it was. I let them do it, because all bullies want is a reaction and if they don't get it they stop bullying.'

'Find your own friends and completely ignore anything anyone else says to you – they're not worth your worries.'

'I think the best way to get through being bullied is try and be confident in yourself and be thankful for who u r, and take no notice of wot others say.'

'Concentrate on the nice things people have 2 say about u, after all that's the only thing that matters!'

'I have managed to survive bullying in a number of ways: 1) Stand up for yourself. Make them feel threatened, but don't lower yourself to their level and start bullying. 2) Ignore them, the bullies will only continue if you don't ignore them. 3) Finally, don't

let them get to you. The bullies will taunt you even more if they know they are getting to you.'

'Stand up to the bullies. Don't walk past them with your head down and a grim face. Walk past holding your head up high and smiling, be confident. Show them they don't hurt you (even if they do). Don't lower yourself to their level, if they call you don't get mad or call them back, just laugh it off and walk away – show them they don't bother you.'

'I get through by just knowing this – as long as I'm not bullying others, the bullies are lesser humans than me. Anyone who is bullied or doesn't bully anyone else is better than all the bullies in the world put together! This gets me through.'

These are some suggestions. Different people find different ways of coping, and you need to find out what is best for you. If things get really bad, you must tell an adult.

AFC LIBRARY

What are the
signs
of stress

Some people can deal with more stress than others, and when the stress does become too much, different people react to it in different ways. Here are some of the signs of stress which people show when things get too much.

● **GENERAL EFFECTS ON YOUR HEALTH**

Dear Doctor Ann, **Can stress make you unhealthy?** Girl aged 13.

Dear 'Can stress make you unhealthy?' – Stress has both good and bad things about it. On the good side, stress can help make us take action and look at things in new ways. We may get stressed when going to a new school or getting into a new relationship – we just have to adjust to these new stresses and learn by our experience of them. On the bad side, stress can make us feel rejected, angry and depressed, which in turn can lead to health problems like headaches and not sleeping. But it can also cause you health problems if you start smoking, drinking alcohol and taking drugs because of stress! So yes – a lot of stress can make you unhealthy, but a bit of stress can be good for you too.

Dear Doctor Ann, **Stress – it pulls your hair out and drives you up the wall, it can even make you fat, but some stress can be good for you.** Girl aged 14.

Dear 'Stress pulls your hair out and makes you fat' – Yes, it can do those things, but a little bit of stress can also be good for you. I don't actually think that many people do pull their hair out with stress, though there are a few people who react to it by fiddling with their hair and pulling a little out. And you are quite right that some people who are stressed do tend to go in for what is known as 'comfort eating', where they eat cakes and other fattening foods because they find it helps keep them calm. Not very good for your health, I would agree, but on the whole better than smoking, binge drinking or taking illegal drugs!

Dear Doctor Ann, **I am constantly worried there is something wrong with me. I always seem to go to the doctor and things always turn out fine. I don't want my doctor to get annoyed with me because it is always nothing. Am I paranoid or just stressed?** 17 year old boy.

Dear 'Constantly worried that there is something wrong with me' – I do hope that your doctor won't get annoyed with you, even if it does mean that you are a bit of a hypochondriac – a bit of a teenage health freak! If you think that there is something wrong with you, your doctor should be spending time talking to you about your fears, and trying to find out what is wrong with you. Then, if you need it, she should be helping you with these things by referring you on to either a counsellor or a psychiatrist. If you are not happy about the way that your doctor is handling it, you can always ask for another doctor to see you.

Dear Doctor Ann, **Hey! Does stress affect your body like, permanently?? When I start to get stressed, any little thing will get me worse.** 12 year old girl.

Dear 'Does stress affect you permanently?' – The answer is 'not necessarily'. We all need a bit of stress in our lives. A challenge creates stress, and everything new that you face in life has an element of challenge about it. If you can manage fairly mild challenges like moving to a new house, or going to a new place for a holiday, or having to make new friends, it helps you to deal with greater challenges or stresses when they come along – like a friend rejecting you, or a relationship busting up. The problem with stress is when it comes so hard that you can't cope. Some people think that if you are stressed long term over many, many years, you do tend to suffer from high blood pressure and more heart disease when you are quite old – like 50 or more. But there is not much evidence that this actually happens.

Dear Doctor Ann, **If u r stressed can it lead to a fit? I had a fit that lasted 30 mins. It happened at Halloween and at Christmas when I had my exams coming up.** 15 year old girl.

> *Dear 'Can stress lead to a fit'* – The answer is 'only if you have a tendency to have fits in the first place'. If all other things are perfectly normal, then stress is not going to make you have a fit. But if something else is wrong with you and you are stressed about something like exams, then yes, stress may bring on a fit.

● HEADACHES

Dear Doctor Ann – **I'm fifteen and I get these headaches which come on when I'm stressed. But what worries me is that I get these funny spots in my eyes and then the headache begins and it's just one part of my head, and I feel sick. Do I have a brain cancer or something?** 15 year old boy.

> *Dear 'I get these headaches'* – It is most likely that you are getting stress headaches, because these are the commonest. It could be migraine, which often runs in families – does you mum or dad or anyone else in the family get them? Migraines do come on with stress and can start with a funny kind of lines in front of one of your eyes. The headaches are usually one-sided and last for an hour or two, but can last longer. Feeling like throwing up is also common. So relax – your headaches are NOT brain cancer. You can suffer from migraine headaches for years, or they may just disappear. There is a large range of medicines which can help with stress headaches and migraine, but if paracetamol doesn't help, then it would be a good idea to go and see your doctor.

Dear Doctor Ann, **My girlfriend gets migraines. She has had one now for 2 months. The doctor did tests and they turned out normal. If there is nothing seriously wrong why has she had pain for so long. Could it be stress?** Boy aged 17.

Dear 'My girlfriend gets migraines' – Yes, it certainly could be stress. Headaches of all kinds may be caused by stress, but particularly migraine-type headaches. There are medicines which she should be able to take to help relieve her migraines, and she can check these out with her GP. But it might also be a good idea to see if she's willing to do some of the things suggested in chapters 9 and 10 to try to prevent getting stressed.

● **DRINKING, SMOKING, TAKING DRUGS**

Dear Doctor Ann, **I know I suffer a lot from stress but just tiny little things can trigger it off. Since this began I have started smoking and drinking a lot; even trying out different drugs. How can I stop?** Girl aged 16.

Dear 'Smoking, drinking and trying drugs because of stress' – What you are showing are very common signs of stress, which many adults as well as teenagers show when things get difficult. It appears to be the actual action of smoking which helps calm people, while it is the nicotine in

cigarettes which keeps people smoking, because tobacco in all its forms is so highly addictive. Drinking alcohol offers a form of release from stress because it helps blot out memory of the stresses – as well as memory of everything else!

Drugs can have variable effects, though, because even cannabis, as well as some of the other illegal drugs, can just make you feel more of what you are feeling anyhow – so if you are already very anxious, smoking cannabis can simply make you more anxious. You also say that you suffer a lot of stress over just 'little things'. There are undoubtedly some people who are naturally more anxious than others, just as there are some people who are taller than others, but unlike being too short or too tall, there are things that you can do to help control your stress – without resorting to smoking, drinking too much and taking drugs. A good start is writing down all the things that stress you, avoiding situations in which you get stressed, or just dealing with one stress at a time. There are lots of other things to do which are suggested in chapters 9 and 10. But do just try dealing with one stress at a time – trying to give up smoking, drinking and drugs will all take a great deal of effort, and need to be tackled when you have managed your other stresses.

● HARMING YOURSELF

Dear Doctor Ann, **I think I get really stressed quite easily. I want to control it as I think I might hurt myself.** Boy aged 13.

Dear 'Think I might hurt myself because of stress' – Yes, some young people do find the stress in their lives so difficult to manage that they think about hurting themselves. Most people, when they talk about 'hurting themselves', mean either cutting themselves or, much worse, trying to kill themselves. It happens when you can see no way out of your problems or escape from your feelings. If these are your feelings, then you need help from other people – NOW! Have you talked to your parents about the way you feel? If you can't talk to them, then what about a teacher who you can talk to at school, or the school nurse? Otherwise there is always your family doctor, who can help you in lots of different ways. But do something about it now.

Dear Dr Ann, **why do people cut themselves?** Girl aged 14.

Dear '*Why do people cut themselves*' – It is usually because it helps them relieve an unbearable feeling of anger, frustration, tension or stress. People who cut themselves (and it is much more common in girls than boys) usually feel that they have to scratch or cut their arms – usually the inside of their forearms. They may use scissors, knives, pins or razor-blades. Frequently people who cut themselves find it hard to express their feelings in other ways, and they find that cutting also draws attention to their problems. It is best to get help from the school nurse or your doctor. It is not a good idea just to rely on help from your friends, as it may make them feel very anxious and stressed themselves. The best thing to do is to make a list of things to do instead, when you feel like cutting, such as going for a walk or preparing a meal. Most people gradually grow out of it and find other ways of expressing their feelings.

Dear Ann, **how do I help getting stressed over my ex boyfriend? I loved him. We went out for ages and it's just ended.**

I don't know what depression is but my mates say I've got it as I have been saved from overdoses and cutting myself. I hope I can get over him. Help me please. 15 year old girl.

Dear 'Stressed over ex boyfriend' – I am so sorry – there are few worse emotional stresses than finishing a relationship with someone you feel you really love, especially if you have been going out together for ages. There are no easy ways to ease the pain, though the pain will ease by itself, especially when you meet someone else who you really fancy. It may feel as if you will never meet someone like him again, but it will happen and it will take time. Meanwhile, I suggest that you write down all the things you enjoy doing most, and arrange to do one or more of these each and every day. That way, you can spoil yourself and won't have time to feel too sad.

GETTING VERY ANGRY

Dear Doctor, how do other people handle stress? I am getting very mad and cannot cool down. 13 year old boy.

Dear 'Getting mad and can't cool down' – Quite often getting angry is caused by actual problems which we can't always escape from and can't always deal with. Not all anger under these circumstances is necessarily bad – getting angry is quite a normal reaction in some situations. But being overwhelmed by anger and not being able to calm down won't solve your stress problems. You need first to think how you can avoid stressful situations, and the best way of doing this is to increase your awareness of what you get stressed about –

by writing down all the situations that stress you. As you won't be able to avoid getting very mad from time to time, you also need to know how to deal with your anger. There are three main ways – expressing it, suppressing it, and trying to calm yourself down. Expressing it is probably the commonest way that most of us use – shouting and swearing, that sort of thing, but you can't lash out at every person or every thing that annoys you. You can suppress your anger by holding it in, then stopping thinking about it, and finally focusing on something else that is positive. There are, however, dangers in not outwardly expressing how you feel, because bottling things up can lead to other problems. Perhaps the best thing to do is to try to calm yourself down when you get really stressed and worked up. You can do this by:

- breathing in and out very deeply, using your tummy as well as your chest;
- very slowly repeating calming words to yourself like 'I must relax', 'I must relax' over and over again while you are doing your deep breathing;
- thinking about some experience that you have had that you found relaxing, like lying on a sunny beach somewhere nice;
- doing some mild form of exercise that relaxes your muscles and makes you feel calmer.

● BINGE EATING

Dear Doc – when I get stressed I eat and eat and eat, and then feel 'gusted with myself and make myself throw up by stuffin my fingers down my throat. I reckon it happens about three or four times a week. What should I do? Girl aged 15.

Dear 'Eat and eat when you're stressed' – It sounds as if you have what is called 'bulimia'. The common thing that happens is that something like stress triggers you off into gorging yourself on all those delicious things like cakes and biscuits and chocolate and stuff. Sort of 'comfort' eating. But then you feel disgusted with yourself and make yourself vomit. But the trouble is that you never vomit up everything that you have taken down, and that means that you also tend to put on weight. Many people binge, then go on to be so disgusted with themselves that they become anorexic, and that is much more difficult to stop. So try to find ways of dealing with your stress other than eating yourself sick. First, write down those things which are stressing you and try to avoid situations where you get stressed. Next, when things get too much, find other distractions, like going for a walk or ringing a friend. As far as eating is concerned, make sure that you sit down to regular meals with your family. You need to get proper help from the school nurse or your doctor before it becomes too much of a habit.

3 Exam stress

There are very, very few of us who don't get stressed about exams, but it is certainly worse for some people than others. But the good news is that there are well-tried things that you can do to help overcome this stress and panic. These will be a great help to you if you are one of those stressed panickers!

• STRESS WHEN REVISING FOR EXAMS

Dear Dr Ann, **I am sitting my highers just now and am finding it hard to concentrate. I have regular breaks in my studying but still can't concentrate. Is there any medicine I could take to help me.**
Age: 16 Sex: male

Dear 'Person sitting highers but can't concentrate' – I'm afraid medicines are not going to be the answer, but there are things you can do. You probably need to do a bit of planning of your work. Divide the work you have to do into small sections and decide at the beginning of the day what you plan to do, making sure you include some easier as well as harder subjects. Don't plan to do more than is possible or you'll always feel you are failing, which will make you depressed and stop you working. Only work for 50 minutes at a time, then take a 10-minute break – go for a quick walk, have cup of coffee, chat to a friend – before starting again. Good luck.

Dear Doctor Ann, **I'm really stressed about exams and I go to a very academic school. Please could you give me some revision tips?** Girl aged 11.

Dear 'Really stressed about exams' – You may want to begin by asking yourself the question why you are so stressed by exams. Who are you afraid of letting down? Is it yourself, or your parents, or do you feel that you will be shown up in front of your friends, or what? Now the best way of standing the pressures is to stay on top of the work. Some of the ways you can do that are...

- work out a clear revision plan and write it down
- get help from your teacher about how to revise
- stay on one subject only for an hour at a time
- make condensed notes as you go along, which will help you when you want to quickly go back over what you have done
- take short rests during your time of work and revision
- plan your work and try to revise at times when you know you will work at your best
- try to stay healthy and get enough sleep
- take exercise – it doesn't matter what, just whatever you enjoy, like walking, running, etc.

- think positively about the future
- try to do your best, as no one can ask you to do more than this
- when the exam is over, don't check it out with friends – it won't make any difference to your result, as what is done is done

---

Dear Doctor Ann, **can stress make allergies worse cos I've got my GCSEs coming up and my allergies seem to be getting worse.** 15 year old boy.

Dear 'Person with allergies and stress with GCSEs coming up' – You may not be surprised to know that stress makes most things worse. Or at least the stress may mean you cope less well with the runny nose, sneezing and itchy eyes that the allergies might be causing. If your allergies are due to pollen, they will be particularly bad when the pollen count is high after sunny weather. Unfortunately exams are often held in the summer, when people's allergies are usually at their worst. But do get some help with the allergies from your doctor and check out ways to help manage your stress – though it will be impossible to get rid of it completely until after your GCSEs.

Dear Doctor Ann, **I am dyslexic and the school doesn't seem to care. Will it affect my exams as I am getting stressed about it.** Boy aged 14.

Dear 'I am dyslexic' – How badly your examinations are affected really depends on how dyslexic you are. Dyslexia means that you have particular difficulty reading and spelling and that the rest of your development is normal. Many people who are otherwise very clever have this problem, and they still seem to be able to manage OK. The thing to do is to get a report on your dyslexia from the person who did the assessment of it and made the diagnosis. You should then make sure that your teachers have the report so that they can take your dyslexia into account when marking your exams. If it is your GCSEs, they need to send the examiners the report as well.

● STRESS JUST BEFORE THE EXAMS START

Dear Doctor Ann, **How can I cope with stress and panic attacks close to my exams?** Girl aged 16.

Dear 'How can I cope with stress and panic close to my exams?' – Almost everyone, unless they have nerves of steel, feels nervous before exams. It may take the form of worrying thoughts about whether you will be able to answer any of the questions, and you may have other things happen to you like getting a lightness in your tummy. Too much of these kinds of thoughts can block your mind and lead to you panicking – which will NOT help! So what can you do? Well first, before the exam you may have already discovered what helps you personally to relax – maybe listening to music, taking a long hot bath, or listening to a relaxation tape. Next, find out as much as you can about the purely practical side of the exam – what the schedule is, where the exam is taking place, how long it will take to get there, what you need in the way of writing implements, all that kind of thing. Next, put yourself in a positive frame of mind by thinking about how you would like the exam to go, rather like rehearsing a part for a play. You can also try doing some practice exams under exam conditions, just to get the feel of

31

how to cope and to make sure that you know how to do the required number of questions in the allotted time. Oh, and don't work at the last very minute before the exam, as it will leave you muddled and anxious.

Dear Doctor Ann, **How can I get my parents to understand how stressed I get with my exams just about to come on?** Girl aged 16.

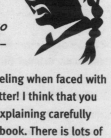

Dear 'How can I get my parents to understand how stressed I get?' – Yes, parents can be really bad at understanding how their children are feeling when faced with exams – or other pressures, for that matter! I think that you should try to get them on your side by explaining carefully how you feel and by showing them this book. There is lots of advice in this chapter about how to deal with your stress, and if your parents read about it all, they will be in a better position to help you do some of the things that are here.

Dear Doctor Ann, **Why do I get ill with diarrhoea when I go into exams? My mum says it's stress but I don't believe her.** Girl aged 15.

Dear 'Getting diarrhoea when going into exams' – Your mum is right. People don't just get 'butterflies' in their tummy when they are about to take exams, they can also get diarrhoea. The reason is that the panic feelings of stress before exams release substances in your body which make your intestines work more actively, and this is what gives you the diarrhoea. The best way of stopping this from happening is to learn how to relax before exams. You need to find out for yourself what helps you relax, as it is different for different people. Some people like listening to music, others going for a walk or having a long hot bath. Experiment and see what happens.

● **STRESS DURING THE EXAMINATION ITSELF**

Dear Doctor Ann, **I've got a real problem 'cos I know the stuff for my exams but I never finish all the questions 'cos I am in such a mess during the exam that I can't get it together enough.** Boy aged 16.

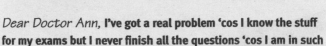

Dear 'Can't get it together during exams' – Try the following. During the exam itself, when you sit down in the examination room, take a long deep breath and focus your mind carefully on the positive thought '**I CAN DO THIS EXAMINATION**', and then breathe out. Take another deep breath and then breathe normally. Make sure that you really, really read the paper VERY carefully before doing anything else. Then mark the questions that you think you can answer and read them again carefully. In order to make sure that you have time to answer all the questions, take the total amount of time you have left for the exam (say 100 minutes) and divide it by the number of questions that you have to answer (say 5), and make sure that you ONLY spend the right amount of time on each question (20 minutes in this example). Jot down quick notes about the thoughts that come into your mind about all the questions that you are going to answer on a separate piece of paper. If you start to panic during the exam, refocus by going back to taking deep breaths and thinking positively. Taking five minutes out to do this may save you from spending the rest of the exam in a panic.

Dear Doctor Ann – **I just panic during my exams. Is there anything that I can do about it as I think it is affecting my marks badly.** 16 year old boy.

Dear 'Panicking during exams' – Here are some tips...

• **Stop negative thoughts.** When you panic at the beginning of exams, it is very easy to have negative thoughts. So in the exam, when you are very anxious or in a panic, you may find yourself saying things like 'I can't do this', 'I am hopeless', 'Help, I am going to give up now'. But you need to say to yourself 'STOP these thoughts' and start thinking instead things like 'I can manage this OK', 'It's going to be all right', 'I know what I'm doing', 'I can do well at this'.

• You might try wearing something, or having something in your pocket, which you like and which you associate with something or someone you feel good about – something like a tiny teddy bear given to you by your boyfriend or girlfriend. Touching it from time to time will give you a good feeling and help comfort you. Then you can allow yourself a few moments to think about your boyfriend or girlfriend, and this should have a calming effect on you.

• Some people find that by giving themselves a mild pain, like squeezing one of their fingers hard or digging a fingernail into the palm of their hand, they can block out the feelings of being anxious or stressed. Others use a rubber band around their wrist, which they twang gently against their skin. You can try and see if this works for you.

- You can try focusing your mind on something else for a bit to distract yourself, like counting the number of lights in the room or the number of people. Other people recite a specific word or phrase to themselves over and over again...like 'I can do this', 'I can do this', 'I can do this'. It is all a way of distracting yourself from your worries for a bit so that you can calm down.

Different things work for different people, so it's worth trying these things out and seeing which is the right one for you. And it is a good idea to experiment a bit before the actual exam itself.

4 Family stress

Not all families are necessarily 'happy families' all the time. All the different family members – parents, step-parents, brothers, sisters, half-brothers, half-sisters – relate to one another in different ways in different families. These relationships can be wonderful, but at times they can be extremely stressful too!

● IT CAN BE THE WHOLE FAMILY

Dear Doctor Ann, **When I feel stress it is because my family sometimes don't understand me but I try to understand them and behave properly so that they don't get at me. But I feel really stressed. What can I do?** 14 year old girl.

Dear 'Stressed by not being understood by your family' – You seem to be taking a very mature approach to this by trying to understand what your family want and behaving properly so that they don't 'get at you'. But I also understand that you are at an age when you may want to be more independent and do your own thing. This may mean that you also expect your family to be more responsive and understanding of your needs? Maybe the time has come for you to have a two-way conversation with them so that you can explain the way that you feel. Your parents may say that you are too young to have the kind of independence that you want, but you will, by opening up negotiations with them, at least start decreasing the stress. It will also help them to see where you want to go and what the problems are – and that's a good beginning.

Dear Doctor Ann, **I hate my family...my sister left when she was 18, my other 2 sisters disown each other. My mom tries to make my younger sister's life hell. My older sister is her favourite. My dad is a recovering alcoholic. I'm stuck in the middle of everything and I'm on the edge of just flipping out. Boy aged 16.**

Dear 'I hate my family' – It will be obvious to you that all families are not necessarily happy families. In fact there is an infinite variety of ways in which family units function – or don't function, for that matter. You need to find some stability outside your family, and this means finding friends who you can rely on. This may take quite a lot of work on your part, because it doesn't sound as if your experiences of relying on other people have been particularly good – but please don't give up. You need to find someone in whom you can confide your deepest feelings about life. It may be a teacher, or a relation, or just a close friend. But being able to tell someone about the way you feel about things – not just about your family, but about your life, work and everything else – is vitally important for you to be able to function normally. Do you have anyone to turn to, someone close enough to trust in this way?

Dear Doctor Ann – I feel really low and I'm having trouble with my parents. I really feel like killing myself and my boyfriend is the only person stopping me. I've talked to my doc and he said I've just got to shut up and put up with it. PLEASE HELP ME!! Girl aged 15.

Dear 'Person thinking of killing yourself because of parent trouble' – I am really, really sorry that you feel so badly about life – especially if it is your parents who are the problem. Great that your boyfriend is so supportive, but you also need professional help. Why not also try writing down the way that you feel? If you can't show this to your parents, then show it to a family friend or a teacher who you like, and discuss it with them. I am also really sorry that you don't feel that your doctor is helpful. You can ask to see another doctor in the practice if there is more than one. Please, please don't give up trying to find help.

Dear Doctor Ann, is there anything I can do to make me feel less stressed? I just feel like I'm ignored all the time 'cos my parents pay more attention to my brothers. Girl aged 12.

Dear 'Stressed because your parents ignore you' – Have you tried talking to your parents about the way that you feel? If you can't talk to them, what about someone else in your family? Is there an aunt or uncle you trust and respect who you feel able to talk to? They may have more time to listen to you about the way you feel. In a big family, it is very easy to feel ignored, particularly if both parents have to go out to work, which frequently happens. You could talk to your brothers, as they may feel that they are not getting enough attention either. Sometimes parents  have to concentrate their attention on one of their children at a time, when they especially need help. Your turn may yet come!

Dear Ann, **I h8 my mum and dad, they make me stress out all the time. What should I do?** Boy aged 14.

Dear 'Hating your mum and dad because they stress you' – I am very sorry to hear this, because we all need our parents. This need is not just for them to provide the food in the fridge and a room for us to sleep in, and to pay for the phone so we can ring friends, but also to have love, respect, friendship and affection for us. You are not going to be able to change your parents (though I often suspect that children would quite like to do this from time to time!), so you are going to have to learn either how to cope with the stress of living with your parents, or how to stop them from stressing you out so much. Why don't you write down all the things they do that stress you? Then say to them, 'Look, I know I must be a stress to you sometimes – tell me what it is I do that stresses you, and then I will tell you how you stress me. Maybe we can see how we can help one another.' I won't pretend this will be easy, but it is certainly worth a try.

Dear Doctor Ann, **It seems like no1 understands why I'm stressed. My mum just has a go at me, and says don't be so miserable. How can I get her 2 understand?** 14 year old girl.

Dear 'My mum just doesn't understand' – Do you understand why you are stressed? It is more important for you to know what stresses you, so that you can deal with the stress, than that your mother understands that you are stressed

– though that is important too. Can you list all the things which are causing you stress at the moment? Also, is it that your mother doesn't understand, or that she just doesn't have the time to listen? You need to pick the right moment to talk to her about these things, when she is not too harassed. Sometimes mothers, who have a lot of things on their mind, are not the best people to talk to about one's troubles, as they may be even more stressed than you. You may need to find someone else who has more time to listen. Do you know some other adult who you like and trust who you could talk to? A teacher, a friend of the family, a relation, the school nurse maybe?

● BROTHERS AND SISTERS CAN KILL YOU

Dear Doctor Ann, **why am I so angry when my little sister is around?** Boy aged 13.

Dear 'Angry when sister is around' – You really need to think about the answer to this yourself. People usually get angry because they feel irritated by something or because something happens which upsets or frightens them. Anger also happens when you are jealous or feel threatened by somebody. Perhaps your sister is causing one of these emotions. If you analyse what is happening, you may be able to put it right by talking about it. If the problem is you are afraid that your parents are giving her more attention than you, try talking to your parents to help sort it out.

Dear Doctor Ann, **Every time when I get back from school I have got an annoying brother who bugs me all the time, so I just shut myself in the bedroom. What do I do?** 14 year old girl.

Dear 'I have an annoying brother' – There are three obvious alternatives. Somehow learn how to get on with your brother, find some way of avoiding him, or do both. The first is better than the second, as he is not suddenly going to disappear completely from your life, and the third way is best of all. No brother or sister should be so aggravating that you have to avoid them all the time though. Have you found any things that you have in common – like hating school, or liking certain kinds of music, or supporting the same football team? You could ask him what it is about you that annoys him, though knowing brothers he may well just answer 'everything!', which will not be much help. On the positive side, you could look at what you do have in common, what you both do like doing together – try concentrating on the positive things!

● STEP-PARENTS CAN BE REALLY TRICKY

Dear Doctor Ann, **I'm 12 years old and I don't seem to get on with my step dad very well! what shall i do!!!** 12 year old boy.

Dear '12 year old who does not get on with his step-dad' – I am sorry to hear this. The most common reason to have a step-dad is because your parents have got divorced, or perhaps your own dad has died. Whatever the reason, it can often be difficult to form a relationship with someone in the house who is your step-dad, not your own dad. You may resent him and feel that he should not be there, and that will not make him feel good towards you either. So there might be worries about getting on with each other from both sides. But it is worth trying to make the relationship work as well as possible both for you and for your mum. Try to work out a way of getting on together and to find things that you like doing together, but don't expect him to be the same as your dad – although in some families this may be the right thing to happen. Try to think more that you have a dad and a step-dad and that they each play a different role in your life. Talk to your mum about it all and try to work something out together.

Dear Ann, **what do you do if your parents are divorced and you don't get along with your new mom but you have to live with her?** 14 year old boy.

Dear 'Don't get along with your step-mom' – About one in every three couples who get married get divorced sometime later. If they have children, then this obviously makes their children very unhappy. And then there is your situation, where your parents are not only divorced but one or both of your parents have got married again. It really should be your stepmother – who is meant to be the grown-up person here – who makes sure that she gets along with you, rather than you having to get along with her. But your stepmother doesn't seem to be very successful at her part of this! First, I think you have to accept that there is not going to be any instant cure and that you need to work at getting things better over a longer period of time. Second, I think you need to think carefully about what is going to be best for you in the long run. How much do you need to put your own needs first, and how worthwhile is it to think about what your stepmother wants? It is not going to be all one way or all the other – you need to work something out between the two of you by talking, rather than just getting angry with one another. You could try showing her this email and asking her if she would be willing to discuss how things could be made better for both of you by talking?

SO CAN STEPBROTHERS AND STEPSISTERS!

Dear Doc, **I have a step brother who me and my brother have to live with. He is the son of my step dad, but he thinks he can rule over us 'cos he is older and me and my brother are living in his house, and I hate him. Help.** 15 year old girl.

Dear 'Living with a stepbrother' – Just because parents decide to get divorced and then remarry someone they fancy certainly doesn't mean that their children automatically fall into one another's arms in friendship. Even natural brothers' and sisters' relationships can be difficult enough. The main thing is that you need to sort this out as a whole family, rather

43

than just seeing it as your own and your stepbrother's problem alone. It is your mother's and your step-dad's responsibility to try to help you and your stepbrother to get on together. Have you already tried talking to your mother about this? Your mum and step-dad can help by listening carefully to the difficulties that you and your stepbrother are having with one another. You also need to realize that in one sense you are in a stronger position, because you have a natural brother living with you as well. You can gang up together, and this may represent a threat to your stepbrother.

Relationship
stress

5

Relationships with other people, especially with friends or with a special boyfriend or girlfriend, can be particularly stressful. We need these relationships and we mind desperately about being liked and loved by others. We depend hugely on our friends to stand by us in bad times and to listen to our problems when they get overwhelming.

● **STRESSED BY FRIENDS**

Dear Doc, **how do you stop getting stressed over friends?** Girl aged 12.

Dear 'How do I stop getting stressed over friends' –

It is sad, but as we all know, friendships can be very stressful. First, there are the friends who want to be our friend and then they want to be someone else's friend, and then they want to be our friend again. It seems that girls especially experiment with doing this. When it happens, it can be very painful and stressful for the person who it's done to. But you should realize that sometimes it is you who are making friends and breaking up with them, and sometimes it is another girl who is making friends and then breaking up with you. The main thing is to keep on trying to make friends, even if sometimes these friendships do end painfully. It is all about learning how to handle life and friends and feelings. So the only way to stop getting stressed is to keep on and on and on trying. It really does come right in the end!

Dear Dr. Ann, I am the most shyest person in the world. I hardly even leave my house for fear of having to talk to someone, and I only have two friends. How can I overcome my shyness and make more friends and get a girlfriend? Boy aged 16.

Dear 'Shyest person in the world' – There are good reasons why people refer to someone who is very shy as being 'painfully shy', because it can be extremely painful and stressful. However, there is probably no one in the world who isn't a bit shy at one time or another. What is shyness? You probably know better than anyone – it is, as you say, an unbearable feeling of not wanting to talk to anybody, especially someone you don't know. It can also be a feeling of great awkwardness and embarrassment, so it is certainly no help when trying to make friends! However, because we all feel shy at one time or another, other people DO understand what you are feeling. The main thing is to find something which you and the person you want to talk to can both talk about. It may be a television program you both saw last night, or football – anything that interests you both. Finding something which interests you both helps 'break the ice' between you. After that first contact everything tends to get much, much easier.

● **STRESSED BY BOYFRIENDS**

AFC LIBRARY

Dear Doctor Ann, **Since I have been going out with my new boyfriend I have been getting very stressed and so have found myself drinking a large amount on very many occasions. What can I do to calm me down? And is it because of my new boyfriend?**
Age: 15 Sex: female

> *Dear 'Getting stressed and drinking too much'* – It sounds as though there is something about this new relationship which is making you feel stressed and that you are using drink to cope with the stress. Unfortunately drinking too much alcohol is not going to help your stress, though it may appear to make you feel more confident. To try and sort out what is really happening, sit down and write down just how much you are drinking, when and why. The best way to find something to calm you down is to find out what is making you stressed and deal with the cause. And that might mean changing the new boyfriend.

Dear Dr Ann, **why are boys always the focus of my life, and why does this stress me so much?** 13 year old girl.

Dear 'Why are boys the focus of my life?' – The answer is basic, the solution not so simple. The reason why boys are the focus of your life is that biologically boys are designed to be attractive to girls, and girls are designed to be attractive to boys. In order for the human race to survive as a whole, people need to have children, and to help us have children, the opposite sexes need to find one another attractive. This mutual attractiveness is stronger in some people and weaker in others. In you, it is obviously very strong. It starts happening around the time you go through puberty and is due to certain hormones beginning to be produced by glands in your body. These hormones tell your brain to find certain features of boys attractive, in both their physical and their mental make-up. These feelings are not going to go away, but they do need to be fitted in with the important things in the rest of your life – your schoolwork, your girl friends, your family and many other things besides. This will happen by itself as life goes on, so don't worry about it too much.

Dear Doc, I'm stressed out every day because my boyfriend comes up to my house every day after school and my mom gets fed up because she said she can't afford to feed him every night and he expects tea here and I feel sorry for him. If I tell him my mom said he can't come up after school I'm scared of hurting his feelings cause he always wants to be with me. What can I say to him please. 15 year old girl.

Dear 'Stressed out every day because of boyfriend' – A difficult situation to handle, but maybe you could use it to your advantage. You obviously understand your mother's problem – not being able to afford to feed him every night and maybe not  wanting to have him around the house all the time. Your boyfriend is not going to be able to understand this by magic, so he does need to be told. It is the way that you tell him that matters. You could make it a special thing between yourselves. Try saying to him something like: 'Look, I wouldn't tell this to anybody else, but because I feel that I really know you and like you, I would like to tell you something rather intimate about our family. My mum really likes you and likes me liking you, so she's giving you lots of food, but she can't really afford it, so could I possibly come over to your house a bit instead?' That way he will feel both that you have told him something special, and that he is able to do something for you by having you around to his house. If he really wants you as his girlfriend, this will make him feel good.

Dear Doctor Ann, I used to go out with this boy and I really liked him. But we broke up and now I can't get him out of my head. I constantly think about him. It's really stressing me out. What can I do because I want him but he doesn't want me. Girl aged 14.

Dear 'Stressed out because of breaking up' – I am so sorry, because breaking up a relationship is always painful, and there never seems to be a right way of doing it. Sometimes it is painful for just one of the two people breaking up, but much more often it is painful for both people. One way of easing the pain would be to talk to one another about it, but obviously that is not possible if he won't see you. It is strange, but many boys find it hard to actually talk about their emotions (the way they feel), so they hide themselves away instead and refuse to see the person they have broken up with. Many girls feel that boys do this because they don't feel

anything, but actually it is the opposite – they may feel a great deal of pain, but sometimes it is so painful that they can't talk about it. I think that you need to be patient and set about finding another boyfriend, so that you can forget the one you have just broken up with.

Dear Doctor Ann, **My most stressful thing are these 2 guys. I know you're thinking 'Oh ur a kid you'll get over it' but what to do when ur pinned between a guy u love and a guy that loves you and wants to marry you. U can't just blow him off b/c he's got depression. I'm 14 and the guy I love is 17 and the one who wants to marry me is 18 and the one I love thinks I that don't. It's just so crazy.** Girl aged 14.

Dear 'Person with 2 guys' – You are certainly learning fast about the complications of relationships. No one can fool you that the world is an easy place when it comes to sorting out relationships. And it wouldn't be easy even if you were a great deal older than you are. It is probably quite flattering for you that your friend with depression wants to marry you, but you

are definitely not the right person to help him with his depression. It sounds as if he may need help from a doctor or a much older person. You should not be tricked into feeling that you have to look after him or give in to him in any way just because he is depressed. The guy that you love and thinks that you don't love him is probably right in that you may be too young to really know what love is, even if you think that you do. I would slow down a bit in your relationships and just keep things at the friendship level. You are much too young to be thinking of any 'marriage' stuff.

STRESSED BY GIRLFRIENDS

Dear Doctor Ann, **can you please help me as I am really confused. I go to an out of school activity called the Duke of Edinburgh. There are a few girls there, but to be honest I thought I had no chance, mainly because I am a bit chubby (not exactly fat) and the girl I fancied most was probably not interested.**

However, when I went on our first expedition and set up camp, I really got to know this girl and I think she began 2 like me as she began 2 see my funny side. However, since the expedition I've hardly spoken 2 her, mainly 'cos we haven't seen each other at the centre much. At the 2nd expedition, our tents were positioned far away from each other, and I didn't have the courage to go up to her and have a general conversation, like we had on the last expedition. I really want to ask her out but I find it really stressful to talk to her, as I easily get embarrassed. I also think she might just reject me and laugh in my face. I've never had a girlfriend before and really do not know how to deal with the situation. Please help. 15 year old boy.

Dear 'Finding it stressful asking a girl out' – You will never know whether this girl will reject you unless you try. If you don't try, then nothing will advance. So you are going to have to (just once) overcome your embarrassment and ask her. You are not alone in fearing that you may be rejected, but believe me, she will feel very flattered and happy that you did ask her, even if she doesn't actually accept you as her boyfriend. It does take a bit of practice to start asking girls you like to go out with you, but every time you do it, it becomes easier. So just start now with this girl who you already know fairly well, and then next time it will be different, because you will know how to handle things better. And each time after that it will get easier and easier.

Dear Doctor Ann, **Why do I get stressed about my girlfriend being with other boys instead of being with me.** 14 year old boy.

Dear 'Stressed about girlfriend being with other boys' – You are probably stressed about this because you are jealous and worried that maybe she will like one of the other boys more than you. This is completely natural, BUT...the best way of dealing with it is to try not to mind. The quickest way of losing your girlfriend is to be possessive of her and to tell her that she can't be with any other boys. You are going to have to learn to trust her – at least a bit. If she betrays your trust, then you can take action, but until then, by far the best thing is to let her be with other boys and to trust that she still finds you special and that she will always come back to you.

6 The stress of illness or someone close dying

Although there are many stresses in life, probably none of them compares with that of dealing with people who one really loves being ill or dying. Death and illness are inescapable parts of life, but can be particularly hard for young people to deal with. They have to be coped with, but that doesn't mean that it is something you have to do alone. And you should never blame yourself for someone being ill or dying.

● SOMEONE CLOSE TO YOU DYING

Dear Doctor Ann, **I get really stressed out. My mum died two years ago and my dad has just opened a shop. It's really not fair plus we moved house. We used to live in Luton but now we've moved to Sheffield. My life is so hard. Boy aged 12.**

Dear 'My mum has died and life is really hard' – I am not surprised that you are finding life really difficult, as you have had two really major losses in your life recently – your mum dying and moving house. Moving house will have meant losing your friends, who might otherwise have been around to support and help you over your mother's death. When someone close to you dies, there are different stages of sadness which most people go through. The first reaction is shock and disbelief that it has actually happened. This can occur even if the person has been very ill and you have been expecting them to die. The next reaction is that after a bit you begin to believe it and stop thinking that the person might come back. This may be followed by feeling rather angry at the person who has died for leaving you. Although this is a perfectly normal reaction, many people feel bad about having these thoughts. When you gradually come to accept your mother's death, you will go on feeling some sadness but it won't hurt quite so badly and life won't be so hard, especially as you start to make new friends. It may be difficult to talk to your new friends about how you feel about your mother's death, so I would suggest that you try talking to the school nurse at your new school. Also try and stay in contact with your friends at your old school – maybe by email – as they will be supportive.

Dear Doctor Ann, **As I have come through my early teenage years I realised that I am often very shy and usually keep my thoughts and feelings to myself. My dad passed away when I was one and my mom had to go to the hospital every day for seven months to visit him and bring him food. This all happened when I used to live in Europe. Could a stress like this affect you at a very young age? I mean my grandma was taking**

care of me when mom wasn't home so it's not like I wasn't raised the right way. Boy aged 16.

> *Dear 'Not knowing your dad because he died when you were a baby'* – Having a parent who dies when you are young – even when you are only a baby – will have an effect on you. Part of this is never knowing that parent and always wondering what they would have been like. Part is just not having one  parent there to help look after you as you grow up. It is very good that your grandmother was able to look after you at that time, when your mother was obviously trying to look after your father every day and therefore would not have been around much to help look after you herself. You may not have thought too much about this until now, but adolescence is often a time when you start to think for yourself and reflect on some of these issues. The reason for your shyness may well be that you have already learnt to keep some of your emotional feelings hidden in case you get hurt. If you feel that you now want to talk about these things, try your mother first, as she may well want to tell you about how she feels about those times. She may also want to tell you what your father was actually like.

Dear Doctor, **I was very close to my grandma. My mum goes out to work and she was always there after school as she lived round the corner from us and my mum is divorced. My friends don't seem to understand because she was very old and they just seem to think that old people die anyhow.** Girl aged 14.

> *Dear 'My friends don't understand how sad I am about my grandmother's death'* – Unfortunately it is

very difficult for some people to understand how upsetting it can be when a grandparent dies, especially if they have not had a close relationship with their own grandparents. It sounds

as though you saw a great deal of your grandmother and were very close to her, so her dying must be a great loss and you probably feel really quite lonely after school. Of course some people feel that 'old people' dying just doesn't really matter as much, because they have to die some time. I think that you should talk about your feelings to your mum, and also ask her if you can have friends around after school.

● ILLNESS IN THE FAMILY

Dear Doctor Ann, **My dad, uncle and my dads mum have a thyroid problem and have to take tablets every morning. I am worried that I will have thyroid problems when I am older because I cannot swallow tablets. Please help.** From stressed 11 year old female.

Dear 'My family have thyroid problems' – It is often the case that thyroid problems are inherited through your genes and therefore run in families. The thyroid is a gland in your neck which produces a hormone called thyroxine. Thyroxine acts on all the cells in your body and affects the overall way that your body works (your metabolism). Sometimes your thyroid produces too much thyroxine, in which case you tend to feel very anxious, your heart beats faster, you get very sweaty, and you lose weight. Sometimes your thyroid gland produces too little, and you feel sleepy, cold and tired all the time. I am not sure which kind your family has, but it is probable that the thyroid is underactive. Don't worry too much about being able to swallow the tablets if you need them, because they are very small and you are likely to learn how to swallow tablets as you get older.

Dear Doctor Ann, **my mum is mentally ill and is being discriminated against by the authorities and that's stressing all of us in our family.** Girl aged 12.

Dear 'My mum is mentally ill and is being discriminated against' – Having someone in the house who is ill is always difficult, but mental illness can be particularly difficult, because the mental health services are not always very good and mental illness can be very unpredictable. There is also the problem that families with a mentally ill person in them can feel that there is something to be ashamed of and that some of the mental illness 'rubs off' on them. But mental illness is just like having any other illness – asthma or diabetes or whatever. You can try talking to your school nurse about the stresses caused by your mum, and maybe she can help you contact social services to get more support. Your mum will have a doctor and a nurse who are responsible for her treatment, and they need to be informed about your stress as well.

Dear Doctor Ann, **Me mum is in a wheelchair. She's got MS and sometimes can't walk. My dad went off so me and my sister have to look after her a lot and feel that we can't go out with our friends which is really stressing us out. Help.** Boy aged 17.

Dear 'Mum is in a wheelchair with MS' – Being a carer is very stressful at the best of times, particularly when you are young and want to be doing other things, and might feel guilty about leaving your mum on her own. You may not only feel stressed and worried but even angry at ending up in this situation. It is important that there is enough support and help for you, your sister and your mum, to make sure that you can do other things which your friends are doing. I am sure your mum would want this too. It is important that you don't miss out on school; that you understand about your mother's illness and what is going on, as this will help; and that you can tell the medical and social services people involved how you are feeling. It is OK to say 'no' to some of the demands that are made of you, so that the adults involved in your mum's care can arrange enough support. Feelings of stress are your brain's way of saying that you need a break. Joining a young carers' club and talking to young people in the same situation may help, as you may find your other friends don't really know what it is like for you. Also, have a look at the *www.youngcarers.net* website.

Dear Doctor Ann, **I'm stressed out coz my grandad is ill. I feel miserable but act loud to cover it up. I am a confident person but I feel it is decreasing my confidence. It sometimes affects my concentration and I feel I am fat but I know I'm not and I want to find a way to relax. I listen to relaxing music which helps and I exercise. What more can I do?** Boy aged 12.

Dear 'Stressed and miserable because your grandad is ill' – I am sure that you are worried that your grandad might die, and talking about his illness and your fears about it may help, even if some of the news is not very good. Being anxious often reduces your confidence, as it can make it hard to do things which you once found easy. This can put you off trying new things

that might be difficult, and then you become even less confident. Some of the things that you are already doing, like listening to music and exercising, are very good. Another thing you might like to try is to write down a list of things that you find completely relaxing, such as sitting in the sunshine, swimming, or going out with friends. You can think some of these 'nice relaxing thoughts' while you do other relaxation exercises. To start with, it is worth trying these exercises in a quiet room by yourself, but with practice you can do them in any situation where you feel tense and anxious. These exercises include breathing slowly and deeply; deliberately dropping and relaxing your shoulders; and consciously relaxing each part of your body from the tip of your hands down to your toes, one bit at a time. While doing this, say to yourself 'relaaaxxx' slowly, again and again. If you have difficulty concentrating and nasty, worrying thoughts keep popping into your brain, start by writing these thoughts down, as well as some nice ones. Then think of throwing away the nasty ones and actually throw the list away. Each time after that that you get a nasty thought, immediately think of a whole lot of nice ones instead.

● A FRIEND HARMING THEMSELVES

Dear Doctor Ann, **What do u do if a friend cuts herself and they really trust you to be quiet about it? Should I tell someone about it, 'cos I'm worried that she'll start cutting again, or should I**

rather just ignore it 'cos she said she'll never do it again. Although it's already happened twice!! I don't know what to do! 16 year old girl.

Dear 'Friend of a person who cuts herself' – You must not feel that you have to take on responsibility for her problem. You must not feel that if she carries on cutting, you have not been a good enough friend. Her stopping cutting has to come from deep within her, and she is likely to need professional help to do this. She may have said to you, 'Don't tell anyone else', but this is not something you can handle alone, and it is very important that you do tell a responsible adult – maybe your mum or a teacher. If she knows that you have done this, she may, at the beginning, feel cross with you, but in the long run, when she is receiving help, she will be grateful. Often, when people say they don't want you to tell anyone, they are actually hoping that you will, because they feel too embarrassed to tell someone themselves. I am not the least bit surprised that you are finding all this upsetting and worrying.

School
stresses

LIBRARY

A good part of life is lived at school, and schoolwork, school friends, bullies and school teachers can individually be very stressful. Put them all together and they can become an overwhelming nightmare! There is no escaping school, so we need to learn how to cope with all these things – both on their own and also when everything goes wrong at the same time, which can happen!

● **STRESSED BY TEACHERS**

Dear Doctor Ann, **I've been really stressed out for the last few weeks because my teachers keep pressuring me because I have potential. What's the best way to sort this out?** Boy aged 14.

Dear 'Pressured because you have potential'
– You are going to have find a balance between what you feel is your potential and what your teachers feel is your potential. It is

absolutely natural that if your teachers (and maybe your parents) think that you can do really well at your schoolwork and your exams, they are going to try to get you to do as well as you possibly can. But I agree that there has to be a balance – too much pressure and you will be unable to cope and to reach your potential, too little pressure and maybe you won't drive yourself hard enough. You are going to have to reach a compromise here with your teachers over just how much work pressure you can manage. The only way to do that is to talk to them about it. Ask them what they are expecting from you, and you tell them what you think you can expect from yourself. With your teachers, set some specific objectives (for example, start with four hours revision per week outside school) that you think that you can manage, and take it from there. With time you may find that you are more and more able to stand up to the pressures of work.

Dear Doctor Ann, **My friend has told me she trusts some of the teachers in school but if she is alone in a room with them she wants to scream and run away from them. Is there something wrong with her?** 17 year old girl.

Dear 'Has friend who trusts teachers but wants to scream and run away' – I think that if I was in a room with a whole lot of teachers, or even doctors, I might feel like screaming and running away at times. But how to help your friend? It sounds as though she is getting acute panic attacks and needs help and support from teachers and probably doctors. Remain a good friend who she can trust and talk to about her feelings, but also persuade her to get professional help. There is something wrong with her at the moment, but she can be cured of these panic attacks with proper advice and help.

Dear Doctor Ann, **There is way too much pressure in schools today. Even in assemblies when the teachers say how great the school is, it puts expectations on you to meet these good images. There should be a place where kids can go just to chill. Do you know any places?** 14 year old boy.

Dear 'Too much pressure in schools today' – Yes, I think that everyone is demanding more and more from young people during their school education. Having such high expectations of young people and pressurizing them into getting the best possible education is one thing, but if young people can't cope or feel that they are failing, then the education system itself is failing. It has to be a careful balance – there do have to be high expectations, but not so high that people feel stressed and unable to cope. Having somewhere to chill out in schools is a good idea. Some schools have a sixth form area where people can go to do this. Also text-messaging friends can help. Taking exercise is another way that some people find useful to chill out. But in the end the best place to find a bit of peace and quiet is 'inside' oneself. That can take a great deal of practice and does need some 'space' in life away from the pressures of work.

● BEING BULLIED AT SCHOOL

Dear Doctor Ann, **I am being bullied every day at school and it is horrible. There is this girl, when I went on a school trip she** started throwing sweets at me and thinking that she was all that. Then ever since she has been calling me names every time I walk past her. 13 year old girl.

Dear 'Bullied every day at school' – I am so, so sorry, and I quite understand how horrible that must be. You need to talk to someone at your school about this. If you don't feel able to do this yourself, you might want to ask one of your friends to do it for you. The questions is 'Who to tell?' You will really have to decide this for yourself, depending on who you think will listen to you best and who will take some action on your behalf. You might decide that this is your form teacher, or the school nurse, or some other teacher you like. The main thing is not to go on taking this behaviour from this girl, but to actually do something about it by telling someone.

Dear Dr Ann, please help. There is a boy in my class who keeps telling me how much he hates me and wants me to die. He won't stop it and he sounds really serious about it. I think he's gonna end up hurting me. I'm going to tell my head of year but there isn't much teachers can do in the long term to stop this kind of stress. I can't ignore him. He speaks directly to me and says it to me from across the classroom when everyone is listening. I feel like dying. 15 year old girl.

Dear 'Feel like dying because of a boy in my class' – There is a great deal that teachers can and will do about it, and you

need to tell them NOW. You may feel that if you tell on this boy, he may make life even worse for you. But don't feel that way. You have to tell a teacher and get them to take action, even to the extent of them moving the boy to another class or keeping him out of school until he stops. But whatever they do is their responsibility, not yours. He is making your life hell, and he must stop it. The only way that is going to happen is by you telling your head of year and insisting that action is taken. If that step seems too much for you, then tell your parents and get them to talk to your head of year.

Dear Doctor Ann, **I am scared of school. I don't know why. I am not getting bullied or anything. I just get scared about the crowds and other kids. I was severely bullied for 6 years and it only stopped two years ago, do you think that my fear could be a long term affect of the bullying?** 15 year old girl.

Dear 'Scared of school but not bullied now' – Yes, your feelings about crowds and other kids may well be left over from when you were bullied. That experience may have left you feeling vulnerable and scared of other people. But if you are not being bullied now, it is a very good time to try and come out of your shell, and to find out that most people are really nice and really kind and that they won't bully you. You will just have to try things out and see what you can manage without feeling scared. Just try talking to someone at school who you think you might like, about something that you are interested in and that you think they might be interested in too. If that goes OK, you can then gradually build up your self-confidence again by extending the number of friends that you have. Don't let a bad experience at school in the past stop you from finding good friends now.

Dear Doctor Ann, **I have real stressful problems with my friends. People are backstabbing me and stressing me about my school work as I can do it and they can't. How can u solve my problem?** Girl aged 14.

Dear 'Being backstabbed by friends at school' – It is often easier to deal with people who are just plain nasty to one's face than people who stab you in the back. Talking about people behind their backs is a particularly nasty thing. I am so sorry that it is happening to you, particularly as it sounds as if they are doing it out of envy because you can manage the schoolwork and they can't. One way of dealing with this is to confront these people and accuse them of badmouthing you, but to do it in front of lots of other people and ask them to stop doing it. At least this brings the whole thing out into the open. It sounds as if they are cowards and certainly won't like being challenged! They will probably deny that they are doing anything behind your back, but you need to challenge that and just say that if they continue to do it, you will tell your teachers and get them to put a stop to it. The one thing that you must do, if you follow this course of action, is to actually tell your teachers if the problem does go on. The other thing to remember is that if these people behave this way to you, they will also be doing it to others. So by challenging them, you may be doing a favour to a whole lot of people, not only improving things for yourself.

Dear Doctor Ann, **Hi! I want to know how I can stop getting stressed out about school work and school things.** 11 year old girl.

> ***Dear 'Stressed out by schoolwork'*** – You are certainly not alone, as there is a greater and greater push on young people to succeed in their schoolwork and in examinations. This does put great pressure on some young people, as it has in your case. I wonder if you have talked to your form teacher about the way you feel? If this is too frightening for you, I would suggest that you talk to your mother or father, and then arrange to go and see your form teacher with them to discuss how they can help decrease the pressures on you. Once you feel less stressed, you will probably be able to work much better.

Dear Ann, **I am only scared of one thing. I can't speak in front of the class room. I get nervous and start to sweat. I say the wrong things and sometimes stutter. I think it's from my prescribed drug for 'attention deficit hyperactivity disorder'.** 15 year old boy.

> ***Dear 'Can't speak in front of the class'*** – I am not sure that it is your prescribed drug for ADHD that is causing you this problem. You have something in common with a great many other people. Your friends in your class may look as if they are quite happy to get up and speak, but believe me they will be quaking just a bit inside when they are doing it. None of us finds it easy to begin with, and it takes quite some practice before it becomes easy. And practice is what you need, but you should do the practice in a situation you feel

comfortable in. If you have a good friend, then why not do a bit of practice with him? If you know that you are going to have to make a presentation to your class, ask your friend to your house and sit him down and go through the piece that you are going to say to your class – again and again and again until you are comfortable with it. If that is too much, you could start with your parents, or ask your teacher if you can practise in front of them. It really is just a matter of time before you begin to feel quite confident, and then you won't stutter. If that doesn't work, talk to the doctor prescribing your ADHD drugs about what you can do and whether it could be the drugs, or whether you need to see a speech therapist.

Dear Doctor Ann, **I feel different from everybody else that is my age. I only know one person that is the same as me and he goes to a special needs school. I'm brilliant at academic work, when I can concentrate, but I get easily distracted. Someone said I might have Attention Deficit Hyperactivity Disorder?** Girl aged 14.

Dear 'Different from everyone else your age' – In school nowadays, with biggish classes, being 'brilliant academically' can sometimes be a problem. Teachers are supposed to make sure that every child gets the right teaching for them, but this does not always happen. And it can be especially difficult if there are disruptive people in the class who distract others who really want to get on with their schoolwork and do well. It is possible that your difficulty over concentration is just because you take things in so fast that you get easily bored. Attention Deficit Hyperactivity Disorder is

difficult to diagnose correctly
and there is still considerable
argument amongst doctors about
how it should be treated. It may
just be that you are easily

distracted for the reasons above, and that you do just need to
work harder and try to concentrate in class. But if this doesn't
work, you could ask your parents to take you to see the doctor
and arrange to have you assessed by an educational
psychologist.

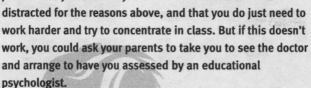

Stressed by
the way
you are

Many, many young people get stressed about the way that nature made them. Too tall, too short, too fat, too thin, too smelly, too sweaty – on and on and on. There are some quite easy things you can do to change the way you are, but there are other things which are impossible to change. So you can't make yourself taller – other than by wearing platforms or having a horrendous operation! Mostly it is a matter of learning to love yourself as you are.

● YOUR WEIGHT

Dear Dr. Ann, I'm told I'm pretty all the time by people I don't know, and I've even been told I should be a model by a modelling agent, but I'm still stressed about my weight and how I look. I eat really healthily and exercise for an hour every day but I haven't seen any changes in my size. PLEASE HELP, all I want is to be fit and happy with myself. 14 year old girl.

Dear 'Wanting to be fit and happy' – You seem to be doing all the right things – eating healthily and exercising for an hour a day. That is very good, as is being pretty. A great many people want either to be a model or to be like a model, but you must remember that in general so-called 'fashion' models are abnormally thin. You are going to have to decide whether you want to go on worrying about your weight and the way you look all the time – which could be a nightmare. Or you could decide just to be fit and happy with yourself and therefore to be something a bit more worthwhile than a neurotic matchstick clotheshorse. Is all that stress really worth it?

Dear Doctor Ann, **I'm a 13 year old boy who eats normally. I eat all my fruits and veggies and I drink my milk and whatnot. I'm also a wrestler and I'm in the 103lbs division. Today I had a match. I usually go to the gym before my matches to sweat off any pound or two because I won't be allowed to wrestle if I'm over 103lbs. Well I was feeling sick yesterday and I didn't wake up early enough to go to the gym today, so I headed to the lockers and weighed in. I was a pound over and I only had an hour before my match started. I tried to sweat it off, but I was still over. So I went to the bathroom and threw up my breakfast. I was then under and I could wrestle. Afterwards, I felt like an idiot for what I did because I knew it was wrong but I still did it anyway. The thought of throwing up my weight before matches has come across my mind several times but I never acted upon it. I don't want this situation to be blown out of proportion, but I'm afraid I'll be in this situation a second time. What should I do if this should happen again?** 13 year old boy.

Dear 'Making yourself sick so that you lose weight' – This certainly doesn't sound like a good idea, but neither does it sound as though it is going to become a real problem, just because you have done it once or twice. If you are desperately keen on wrestling and also desperately keen on wrestling at a specific weight, then you may just have to work harder over a longer period of time, exercising and eating properly in order to keep your weight down, rather than taking the short-term solution of throwing up.

Dear Doctor Ann, I am really stressed. I am a female of 12 and I am 13 stone. My mum says I have the body of a 36 yr old which depresses me. HELP ME!! Dieting is more stressful to me, I do however have a loving boyfriend and I think I have gorgeous eyes. I just get teased bcoz of my weight and my skin (spots). 12 year old girl.

Dear 'Teased because of your weight and spots' – You actually have the best person in the world to help you in your loving boyfriend and you do have those gorgeous eyes. I don't think that your mum is helping much, saying that you have the body of a 36 year old, but she is probably anxious and doesn't know quite what to do. First, I think that you can relax a bit, because many girls get a bit chubby around the time of puberty and then thin out again as they grow taller. Next, you don't really have to diet, and you certainly don't have to diet 'stressfully'. You just need to think a bit about the food you are eating. There is a huge range of really good things to eat which don't contain an enormous number of calories and which do taste delicious. If you want a full list of these, you can look on my website at *www.teenagehealthfreak.org.* Meanwhile, cut out the crisps and chips. The second thing that you can do is take a bit of exercise – just 20 minutes five times a week will help enormously. It doesn't have to be very vigorous – walking or cycling will do.

● THE WAY YOU LOOK

Dear Doctor Ann, **I'm really jealous of my m8 'cos she's really pretty and thin and I'm ugly and fat. I feel sooo out of place when I'm with her especially when I go shopping with my mum. I go in shops and look at nice clothes and try to fool myself that I can wear them but the truth is that I can't look nice in anything I wear!!!!** 13 year old girl.

Dear 'Jealous of mate because she is really pretty and thin' – The bad news is that many girls, around the time of puberty, put on weight and become rather fat. The very, very good news is that over the next couple of years, by eating right and taking a bit of exercise, you will lose weight and become thinner. You will be sooo glad when you are 15, and taller and thinner, and able to get into all those lovely clothes, but do remember to eat healthily and take exercise.

Dear Doctor Ann, **I have bigger breasts than my friends and I feel very, very self-conscious about it when our school goes swimming.** 11 year old girl.

Dear 'Bigger breasts than my friends' – I am so sorry that you feel self-conscious about this. Many girls, after

73

puberty, wish that their breasts were bigger; a few, like you, wish that they were smaller. If your breasts have grown, you have obviously started puberty already. It is likely that many of your friends have not started yet. They  will grow breasts soon and won't be any different from the way you are now, so I think that you just need to be patient. They are probably very envious of the size of your breasts at the moment.

● THE WAY YOU SMELL OR SWEAT

Dear Doctor Ann, **Hi. Please help. I know this may be disgusting but I haven't washed/had a bath/shower for about 5 weeks. I am worried. Could I have done any damage? Is it bad for girls not to have washed the lower part of the body for this long?** 15 year old girl.

Dear 'Haven't bathed/showered for 5 weeks' – There must be a good reason for this. Do you have some other problem, like very sensitive skin – or what? If there is a good reason for you not to have bathed, then don't worry too much. No, I don't think that you will have done any damage. In olden times – hundreds of years ago – many people used not to change their clothes or to bathe or wash for months at a time, particularly during the winter when it was very cold. They probably did smell pretty awful, but you can avoid quite a bit of that by changing your clothes regularly (like once a day). Having said all that, if there is no good reason not to wash the lower part of your body, then it is definitely a good idea to wash down there at least once a day, and maybe even use a deodorant of some kind.

Dear Doctor Ann, **I have a really annoying problem – my armpits sweat way 2 much. I don't fink I have b.o. at least, but it is just really uncomfortable. When i'm out wiv friends trying 2 enjoy myself I am really stressed and conscious about revealing my armpits. Other than having 2 shop about 4 a good deodorant, r thr any 'quick fixes'? I've heard sumwhr that baking soda or something can prevent over sweating, but I'd rather get information from a professional.** 16 year old girl.

Dear 'My armpits sweat way too much' – I am not sure whether you are actually worried about the amount of sweat that your armpits are producing, or the smell of the sweat. I think that it must be the amount of sweat, because you say that you don't think that you have BO, though you might want to check that out with a good friend who is in a position to tell you whether it is true or not. The problem here is that the amount of sweat we produce varies from one person to another, just as some people are taller and some people are shorter. The point of the body sweating is to make sure that the whole of your body stays at the right temperature and does not overheat. You can do some simple things first. Artificial-fibre clothes will make you sweat more, so make sure that you wear natural fibre (like cotton) next to your skin, or wear an artificial fibre which is specifically designed to 'wick' away sweat from your skin (there are quite a few of these around nowadays). The next commonsense thing to do is to wash and bathe yourself frequently, several times a day if you can. Finally, you can try an anti-perspirant which contains aluminium chloride hexahydrate. One that you can buy yourself over the counter is called 'Driclor'. If none of that helps, then I suggest that you go and see your doctor.

● YOUR TEETH

Dear Doctor Ann, **I have a brace and am stressed that when my brace comes out my fillings will fall out as well at the same time, please help.** 13 year old boy.

> *Dear 'Stressed that your fillings will fall out when your brace comes out'* – Although I have never heard of anyone worrying about this before, it does, on the face of it (and sorry for the pun), seem to be a quite reasonable fear. But neither your fillings nor your teeth will fall out when your brace comes out. Teeth are fantastically well stuck into your jaw, as any dentist trying to pull a tooth out will tell you. It takes all their strength at the best of times. Your jaw, your teeth and your fillings will stay exactly where they are, as you will obviously be very glad to see, when your brace finally comes off.

● YOUR SKIN

Dear Doctor Ann, **I have eczema what shall I do because I am really worried about it because it is bad and causes me real probs in my life!** Girl aged 12.

> *Dear 'Eczema suffer'* – I am so sorry to hear about your troubles. The good news, though, is that there are lots and lots of different things that you can do for eczema. Some of them are just straightforward things you can

manage yourself; for others you will need to get some help from your doctor. Eczema is really quite common – it affects about one in every 10 people. It tends to run in families, and people with hay fever are more likely to get it. It normally gets better as you get older. Some eczemas are caused by allergies, so it may come and go depending on what you are allergic to. It may be things which your skin comes into contact with, like washing powder or some kinds of make-up, and then it is just a question of not using those things. Some people get eczema when they eat eggs or certain other things, so again it would be a matter of avoiding those things. But very, very often people get eczema and never know why, so if that is the case with you, the thing to do first is to stop your skin getting dry by using moisturizers. There are a great many available at your local chemist, and you just need to experiment with a few to see which ones suit you best. If none of these things works, then you need to go and see your doctor, who will probably give you an ointment or cream containing steroids. These can have some side effects unless you use them very carefully, so always look at the instructions for their use and only do what they say.

Dear Doctor Ann, **I keep getting more and more little spots on my arms and face and they are really stressing me out. What do I do, please help me out.** Girl aged 12.

Dear 'Have little spots on face and arms' – It sounds as if you have acne. Most of us get acne at

one time or another in our lives, so don't worry. You also shouldn't worry because there is a large number of different creams and lotions which you can try. Get down to your local chemist and see what they have. Something with benzyl peroxide in it is a good starting point. If none of these lotions works, then it would be worth seeing your doctor for some antibiotic lotion or tablets.

How to deal with stress
What young people have to say

By far and away the best advice on how to deal with stress comes from young people themselves. They are experiencing the stress and they know the best ways of coping with it. In this part of the book the advice and experience of young people are given without replies from Dr Ann: all the advice has been emailed to us by young people who have been through the stress themselves.

● TALKING TO OTHER PEOPLE

'I feel it's important that you get some feedback on the subject of stress as it effects so many people nowadays and I feel that reading about similar situations can sometimes help someone else get through this difficult stage. Throughout my secondary school years I had such a terrible time and I didn't feel like I could open up to anyone. It took 1 individual to spoil what's supposed to be the best time of your life. Hardly seems fair does it? Endless times I sat talking to myself, deciding how I would react the next time I came face to face with this monster?! Yet somehow I never followed my actions through and I tried to ignore her torturing comments and endless abuse. It was horrific! I couldn't walk past her without her making a comment or childishly throwing herself into me. Her evil glares made me feel so small and I constantly asked myself why me? I do consider myself to be a decent person – I wouldn't hurt anyone, not even her. But why? She was stabbing at me through her words and actions. She hacked away at my emotions sending them crazy. I was completely trapped. I felt so alone. Still to this day I have never opened up to anyone. I try and hide this terrible time of my life but it will always be with me. Always. It's important to know that you are not alone and somehow there is always a light at the end of the tunnel. It will save you. Remember that!' Girl aged 17.

'You can beat being stressed by always talking to someone – maybe more comfortable talking to friends or one of your own relations.' Girl aged 11.

'I think the best thing people can do when they are stressed out is to tell someone. Whether it's your parents, your friends, etc. It works for me all the time and I hope it will work for others too.' 12 year old girl.

'The best way to handle it is to let it out and tell your brother or sister and see if they have been through the same before, or even try your friends.' Boy aged 14.

'Just try and let a mate know then they can also advise you on how to chill out – it works trust me!!' Girl aged 16.

'I think you should try and talk to someone trusted about your problems because a problem shared is a problem halved! I always found it quite hard to do that at first but when you confide in someone you feel a weight has been lifted off your shoulders and you no longer hold the weight of the world on your back.' 13 year old girl.

'My friend takes his anger out on me everyday at school. He has temper, memory, hearing and eyesight problems. He calls me names and makes me really stressy. I take my anger out on myself sometimes but not very often. Best is that I talk to my dad sometimes and sometimes my friends, which helps me.' Boy aged 14.

● **EXERCISE**

'If I'm stressed I go swimming, which releases the chemicals from my brain.' Girl aged 11.

'I find going for a ride on my pony a good therapy. I do this all the time when I get annoyed but I never beat her or do anything like that. I just get her to work properly.' Girl aged 14.

'If you are stressed, you need time out to think about things, so you should go for a long walk or something to clear your head. Or talk to someone you can trust like your parents or close friends.' Girl aged 12.

● **THINKING YOURSELF OUT OF IT**

'I reckon you should just think of the good things in life and don't let it get to you, or just have a good cry and get over it.'
Girl aged 14.

'The best way I find to deal with stress is to sit on your own for a couple of minutes, think what it is all about and just calm yourself down.' 13 year old girl.

'If you are stressed out then you should go out and do something that you really, really enjoy so as to take your mind off things.'
Boy aged 13.

'Stressing about your work doesn't help at all. I find that if I stress out and worry I end up not doing anything. The truth of it is that if you think something is really hard at school, then everybody else does too. We just have to say to ourselves that we will do our best and that's all that matters.' Girl aged 16.

'Just try to ignore the people that stress u out.' 14 year old girl.

'You need to forget about everything that's going to happen and take things as they come.' Girl aged 15.

'Just tell ya self you can get through tests, SATs etc... and if you are being bullied stand up to them. I found most bullies are all mouth.' 14 year boy.

'I am really overweight and I have found that to be confident It's not about the way you look, it's more about who you are Inside – not outside.' 13 year old girl.

● MUSIC

'If you get stressed just try to chill out. Go up to your room and put on some calming music and when you feel calm enough, go and talk to the person that stressed you out.' Girl aged 16.

'I think listening to music helps. Quiet stuff like Norah Jones chills me out a lot. Maybe you could try it.' 14 year old girl.

'Go upstairs, whip some big headphones on, close ur eyes, lie on ur bed n listen to the best music you have.' Boy aged 14.

BEING ON YOUR OWN

'The best way 2 cope with stress…is probably just to be on your own once in a while, somewhere quiet so you can think.' 15 year old girl.

'If you are stressed out, just chill in your room and watch TV. It works for me.' Girl aged 11.

To avoid stress you should just go somewhere and chill.' 12 year old boy.

WRITE THINGS DOWN

'If I have loads of stuff to do (homework or too much other stuff) then I get REALLY stressed out. To tackle this I write down a list of all the things I need to do to remind me and I cross it off as I do it. It really helps!!!!' Girl aged 13.

'You should sit down and write all your problems out on a piece of paper then rip it all up.' 13 year old boy.

OTHER WAYS

'What do you do if you are getting stressed by being bullied? 1) tell a parent 2) tell a friend 3) tell a teacher 4) tell them to leave you alone 5) just ignore them.' 14 year old girl.

'Take natural remedies, herbal teas, and read lots of good books while listening to a bit of light classical music — that does it for me.' 17 year old boy.

'Keep out of the way of other stressed people.' 12 year old girl.

'There are a few things but the thing that really gets me is when I try 2 train my dog! She mostly listens 2 me but when she doesn't I take it out on her by shouting at her! So I take her on a walk and she suddenly makes me O.K. again. She does it with all my stresses.' Girl aged 12.

'People need to be more understanding when a friend or classmate says they are stressed out.' 14 year old boy.

'If ur stressed go out n live life a little!! if ur parents want u 2 stay in & revise then stay in, but only for 4 nights of the week cuz otherwise it aint fair on u!!' Girl aged 15.

How to deal with stress
What Dr Ann has to say...

There are few of us who get through life without some stress – we would just rather it wasn't thrown at us all at one time! If we are able to deal with little stresses, then we can gradually build up our strength to cope with bigger and bigger stresses. The problem is that when we are young, there are so many new experiences and feelings to manage. As we get older, many things just don't seem quite as important because we have seen them and dealt with them before. But there are good things to do which can help.

● EASY THINGS TO DO

Dear Doctor Ann, **What are the five top things to help stress?** Boy aged 13.

> *Dear 'Stressed'* – Any number of things cause stress. A bit of stress is perfectly normal and something that we all have to

put up with – it probably even helps us get things done! However, too much stress does stop us functioning properly. Here are some tips to help:

- make a list of things that are stressing you
- talk to a friend, your parents or another adult about what is stressing you
- look at the individual things that are stressing you, and only attempt to deal with them one at a time
- do something you really enjoy, to give yourself a break from the things that are stressing you
- take some exercise, as this helps release the natural endorphins in your body, which will help you cope with your stress
- a sixth one for luck – avoid too much caffeine, as in coffee, coke and tea, as too much of it can increase your feelings of anxiety

Dear Doctor, **what music helps you calm down most?** 14 year old girl.

Dear 'What music helps stress?' – This very much depends on each individual. Some people find calm quiet music the best, whilst others prefer loud rap or rock or whatever. Experiment to find out what music is best for you, and then you can also avoid any music that makes you more stressed.

Dear Dr. Ann, **I think that when people get stressed they should have a go on a punch bag – is that OK?** Girl aged 13.

Dear *'Have a go on a punch bag'* – Thanks for this suggestion. I agree that sometimes it can help to deal with stress by punching something. Just make sure it is a punch bag or a pillow or a cushion or something soft, so that you won't hurt yourself when you hit it. Also make sure that it is not another person, so that they won't get hurt or hurt you back!

● WHEN FEELINGS OF STRESS ARE WORSE

Doc – **how do you get rid of horrible memories that you get nightmares about?**
13 old year boy.

Dear *'Having horrid memories that you have nightmares about'* – This sounds serious, and something that you need to talk to someone about over a period of time. Memories serious enough to give you nightmares will finally fade, but they can be eased by talking through your feelings about these memories with a counsellor. And if that doesn't work, you may need to see a psychiatrist. First off, I would suggest that you go and talk to your family doctor.

Dear Doctor Ann, **I get this dark, angry feeling when I'm upset or angry. Maybe it's stress but I really need advice on how to stop this feeling, sometimes it makes me cry. Please help!** 13 year old girl.

Dear *'Dark angry feelings'* – Yes, maybe this is stress. It does sound as though talking to someone about your feelings would help you. Have you tried doing this? Other things that you might find help are suggested by other young people who get really stressed – look at chapter 9. They suggest things like listening to music, going for a walk and writing things down. If your feelings are making you cry, you definitely do need to tell someone else about them, so that they can get you help. It is not good holding these feelings inside you. Other people can help.

Dear Dr, **what should I do when I'm really stressed???** 13 year old girl.

Dear 'What can you do when you get really stressed' – The first thing is to ask yourself, 'Can I avoid getting stressed in the first place?' What is it that is giving you the stress – friends? exams? teachers? overwork? Then you should ask yourself whether you can avoid any of these stresses. Some you will be able to avoid – maybe overwork or certain friends – but many you won't be able to avoid, like exams and teachers. Even more likely is that there will be several different things at any one time that are giving you stress, so a good thing to do is to make up you mind what all the stressful things in your life are and write them down. Then decide that you are going to try and do something about these one at a time. Suppose it is something like not getting enough sleep. Make the decision to go to bed earlier – have a hot bath before bed to help you relax, avoid drinking anything with caffeine in it, and try reading a restful book. If that works, then after a week decide on the next stressful thing that you are going to tackle...say, teachers who are demanding too much: go and talk to them about what you can and can't do. After you have sorted that, move on to the next stressful thing.

Dear Doctor Ann, **How can I stop feeling so stressed out when all I want to do is scream and smash something?** 14 year old girl.

Dear 'All I want to do is to scream and smash something' – Actually screaming is probably not such a bad thing. Some people also find smashing things helps as well, but it is a good idea to be very careful about what you choose to smash and where you smash it. Old china that no one wants smashed outside in the back garden is the safest, but that still may upset your parents, so it is better to try and avoid getting to the stage where you want to scream and smash things. First, you need to understand what all the different things that are stressing you are. It is easy to let a whole range of different things get to you at the same time, and then together they feel so overwhelming that you feel there is nothing that you can do about them. And then it is SCREAM AND SMASH time – because you feel so overwhelmed. Well, if you look at each of the stresses separately, they may be more manageable. Dealing with a little bit at a time will give you a feeling that you are back in control again.

● WHO TO TURN TO

Dear Doctor Ann, **What should you do if you feel stressed and you need to talk to someone other than your mum or a friend?** 15 year old girl.

Dear 'Stressed but want to talk to someone other than your mum or a friend' – There are other people around you who you should be able to trust and talk to about how you feel. There may be someone else in your family who is close to you – an aunt or uncle – or a family friend? If not, have you thought of talking to the school nurse or a teacher? Otherwise, why not go and see your family doctor? If you don't want to go with your mum, you can still arrange to go and see him/her by yourself. You don't have to have your parents with you, and the doctor will keep anything that you tell them secret unless they feel that you are in danger of being harmed in some way. And even then they will discuss who you would like told about it.

Dear Doctor Ann, **What can you suggest because I find that I eat when I am stressed and I want to stop as I am.** 12 year old boy.

Dear 'I find I eat when I am stressed' – Yes, lots of people find that they want to eat when they are stressed. It is probably your body seeking some kind of comfort. For many people chocolate is a particular favourite, and it is thought that chocolate does contain some chemical substances that help stress. The problem, as you already know, is that chocolate also contains a large amount of sugar and therefore, when eaten in large amounts, makes you fat. Another way of dealing with stress is to take exercise. This helps the body to release natural chemicals (endorphins) which help to calm stress, and of course exercise also helps you to lose weight rather than gain it. Pick some kind of exercise which you already enjoy, maybe tennis or walking to school, and just work harder at it. Around 20 minutes of exercise 3 to 5 days a week is meant to be very good for all these things.

Dear Doctor Ann, **A question about stress.... do you know of any medical ways of calming down stressed people?** 14 year old girl.

Dear 'Any medical ways of calming down stressed people' – It depends what you mean by 'medical'. Normally doctors would first recommend that you try some of the self-help methods of dealing with stress. If that didn't work, they might then suggest seeing a counsellor or even a psychiatrist. But yes, there is a whole range of medicines which do calm people, and then there is a whole different set of medicines which help people with depression, though there is quite a lot of argument over whether these work with young people. Some of the medicines to help people with stress do calm people down, but they also make people feel a bit like zombies – they don't have any strong emotions at all, it sort of does away with the 'passions' of life, which isn't always very helpful! A bit of stress is a normal part of life, and we all need to learn to cope with this kind of stress. The better we deal with this kind of stress, the more we are able to cope with the really big stresses, so you don't want to go rushing off to take medicines every time things go badly. But when the stresses are really, really bad – yes, medicines can definitely help.

11

When the stress gets too much to cope with

Although we all feel stress from time to time, there are moments for some of us when it can all get too much. It can happen when just one really, really big thing goes wrong, or it can be a build-up of all sorts of things – maybe against a background of depression. The main thing then is not only knowing where to go for help but also being able to summon up the energy to get that help.

● **FEELING DEPRESSED, FEELING SUICIDAL**

Dear Dr. Ann, I am worried about my brother, he has been really depressed lately and is really upset about his friends annoying him. He has told me he felt suicidal.
Please help!!!! 12 year old boy.

Dear 'My brother has been really depressed lately' – You are doing just the right thing by finding out how to get more help. But if your brother is feeling suicidal, you need to urgently seek some immediate help from those around you. I would suggest that this is a case where, even if your brother has told you to keep it a secret and you have agreed, you should break the agreement. You could try talking to your parents about it first, as they need to be the ones to try and get further help for your brother from the family doctor. If you can't talk to your parents about it, then you need to talk to some adult friend who you trust, like a teacher at school or someone else in your family. But do it now please!

Dear Doctor Ann, **Help me I think I'm depressed because I always feel down and I always worry about my appearance every day and I say what's the point, I'm ugly anyways and I have a sister in a wheelchair and I have to take her to the toilet and sometimes I get really angry at her but I don't mean it!! Also I think that some people don't like me at school and that they say things about me. I'm frightened that I'll lose all my friends. I've thought about suicide. I say 'why don't you just kill yourself?' in front of a mirror sometimes. I did that today but I don't harm myself. I'm too scared so I just think about it. I told my grandma about some of these things but not the suicide thoughts. I said I might be depressed and she gave me a funny look and said you are not. Also I think that I'm going to do something wrong and the**

school will call or my dad will come in and say I've done something. I just don't know what to do. Sometimes I'm happy but there are always points where I feel so low and I have had major family problems as well. Should I see a doctor about this? 15 year old girl.

Dear 'Depressed and thinking about suicide' – You really have a huge load on you and nobody aged 15 should have to bear such stresses. The question is, where can you go to get help? It sounds as if you should first go and see your family doctor and talk to him/her about the way you are feeling. You can go alone if you prefer, and if you want to talk about things that you would rather were not passed on, then all you have to do is say so, and your doctor will keep them confidential. Otherwise you may want to take someone with you – a friend or your grandma or someone else you trust. You should be completely open with your doctor about your feelings, even about getting angry at your sister in her wheelchair, as these feelings are completely normal and your doctor won't be shocked. It sounds as if you need far more support at home with helping to care for your family, and hopefully your doctor will be able to arrange more support for you in your caring role from social services. Please, please take action now and see your doctor.

Dear Doctor Ann, **Hi I get bullied 24/7, it's not fair. I can't stop cutting myself and I tried to commit suicide last night. I took an overdose of insulin as I feel so low at the moment. What shall I do?** 15 year old girl.

Dear 'I took an overdose of insulin' – Get help NOW. The people that will be able to help you are first your parents – have you told them how you feel? Next you could try a trusted family friend or a trusted teacher at school. Tell them the details of how you feel and ask them to get you help. If you can, go and see your doctor and ask for help. The fact that you tried to take an overdose of insulin suggests that you are diabetic, in which case you must be seeing a medical person who is overseeing your care. Have you told them about the way you feel? Feeling suicidal is just like being ill – having pneumonia or whatever. You need to get urgent help with your particular depression problem. There are cures – why not get them NOW and stop your suffering?

Dear Doctor Ann – **I am in foster care and I feel depressed, so that I cut my body in temper to release my stress – can you give me some advice?** 13 year old girl.

Dear 'Stressed and depressed in foster care' – I am so sorry to hear about your troubles. Poor you. You haven't said why you had to go into foster care. Something must have gone wrong that you can't be with your own parents, but you may have some wonderful foster parents. Or are there things upsetting you and making you depressed where you are in your foster care? Try to find an adult you can trust and talk to about these problems – a teacher, a doctor, a good friend, a relative. If none of these is available, what about phoning ChildLine and talking to them? Their number is 0800 1111. It is quite common for young people to cut themselves to release tension. It usually doesn't mean that you want to kill yourself, though.

Dear Doctor Ann, **I'm really confused. I think I could be depressed or something. I used to be anorexic for a while and got very skinny but now I seem to be overeating and indulging myself when I'm not even hungry. I want a way out of this, I'm sick of it.**

I would just like to stick at 9 stone and stay there. I went on holiday and put half a stone on and now I have put even more on because of binge eating. I feel very upset and depressed and often cry about being so fat and disgusting. 14 year old girl.

Dear 'Depressed, was anorexic and now binging' – The pattern of being anorexic and then binge eating is called bulimia and is really quite common in girls. What happens is that, when you become anorexic, you set very strict rules for yourself about what you can and cannot eat. These rules are usually so strict that you can't stick with them because you feel so hungry. So you break the rules by binging on everything you can lay your hands on. Then you vomit and try to get rid of all those extra calories that you have just taken in. But the truth is that, however much you vomit, you cannot get rid of more than half the calories that you took in during the binge, so people with bulimia tend not to lose weight. You really, really need to ease up on the dieting and think of other ways of keeping your weight at a sensible level (nothing extreme, remember). The best way is to eat healthily, which simply means including in your diet each day five portions of fruit and veg – five in all, not five each! This will fill you with good stuff and help hold off feelings of hunger, so you won't eat too much of anything else. At the same time you need to take some exercise. Nothing drastic, like running marathons, but just build in about 20 minutes of walking, swimming or some other form of gentle exercise five days a week. The exercise will not only help keep your weight down by burning off the calories but also help your feelings of depression. The main thing, though, is to stop being obsessed about your weight and get on with the rest of your life.

Dear Doctor Ann, **I'm a teenage boy and as most parents say 'boys will be boys' but I have found that my behaviour has become very bad. I used to be quite a nice person but now I fight and do lots of bad things which I regret later. For example I set fire to a house, but the sick thing is, at the time, I liked doing it! Is this just teenage behaviour or more a stressed case?!!** 14 year old boy.

Dear 'My behaviour has become very bad' – No, setting fire to a house is not normal behaviour by any stretch of the imagination. Nor does it sound like you are a 'stressed case'. It does sound as if you are going over the top with testing the world for what it will stand in the way of your bad behaviour, and the answer is 'it won't stand it', and somewhere along the line a disaster will occur. Please, please do not go on testing things to destruction. You really need to talk to someone close to you about your feelings about what you are doing, because you obviously know it is wrong. You could try a close family friend first, who you trust, but otherwise I would suggest that you see your doctor and arrange to get some counselling. Talking to someone confidentially about your deepest feelings about what you are doing would be a very good beginning.

How *not* to deal with stress

12

It can be tempting, when really stressed, to use short-term fixes. This is easy to understand, but the problem is that it can, in the long run, just lead to further stresses and into a spiral of things getting worse and worse. The best thing is to try and avoid getting into this situation by seeing what is happening and taking action before you start on drugs, alcohol or smoking.

● TAKING DRUGS

Dear Doctor Ann, **I am naturally a stressed out person but lately I have been smoking a lot of weed to calm my nerves but the next morning everything bothers me again so again I smoke more weed. What can I do to get out of this cycle. I think that I am losing my memory and sanity because of it.** Girl aged 17.

Dear 'Naturally stressed-out person smoking a lot of weed' – You are at least on the way to helping yourself by realizing that smoking

cannabis is not the answer to your problems! Perhaps you have been reading the recent evidence that cannabis may cause people who have a tendency to mental health problems like psychoses to get worse. It is sort of swings and roundabouts nowadays with cannabis use. The government has decided to decrease the seriousness of the penalties for smoking cannabis, but at the same time there is more and more evidence of the harm it might cause. Given the number of people who smoke cannabis and the number who smoke tobacco and the health problems caused by tobacco, it would be logical to bring in penalties for smoking tobacco rather than to decrease the penalties for smoking cannabis! However, you need help with your stress in order to break the cycle of cannabis use, and yes, cannabis does cause memory loss as well as being associated with mental health problems. So you need to think about other ways of dealing with your stress. The first thing is to work out the causes of the stress and try to avoid them. Then you can take action, such as taking exercise, talking to people about your stress, and even seeing what your doctor has to offer.

Dear Doctor Ann, **I've been told loads of times that taking too many paracetamol at once and over a long time can damage your liver and kidneys. I used to try to overdose on them and took 10 at any one time several times and then I got addicted so I kept taking between 3 and 5 a day because I was so stressed and it helped. But what sort of damage could have been done? I'm quite often tired and have really bad headaches if I don't take them and stomach cramps. Could this be because of the paracetamol?** 15 year old girl.

Dear 'Taking too many paracetamol because of stress' – The simple answer is absolutely yes, taking too many paracetamol over a long period of time (or a lot over quite a short period) can damage your liver and kidneys. You need to stop now and go and see a doctor to discuss how to deal with your stress in a better way. If you are so stressed that you are having to self-medicate to cope with it, then you need proper help and you need it now. By proper help I mean seeing a doctor who can refer you on to a specialist. Not being able to cope with your stress is just like being ill, and there is a range of treatments that you can get via your doctor. So go and see your doctor urgently!

DRINKING ALCOHOL

Dear Ann, I am always stressed out every day. Drinking calms me down but I only take that if I am stressed. I really do want help because I want to know why I am always stressed over little things that bother me! 15 year old girl.

Dear 'Want help with being stressed over little things' – You first need to decide for yourself why you get stressed over little things. We all get stressed over big things, like people we love getting ill, breaking up with a boyfriend or girlfriend, losing a whole lot of money – that kind of thing. But we don't all get stressed over little things, like no butter for the toast in the morning, or can't find my shoes, or why does it have to rain again today? There may be a whole range of background problems in your life which you are not really facing up to, and then along comes a little thing – your younger brother shouting at you – and pop! you go berserk and act quite unreasonably. Drinking alcohol is certainly no way to deal with stress, particularly because if you drink too much, your background stress may make you behave entirely erratically and even violently. First, try and think very carefully indeed about what it is that Is actually causing you stress. Don't necessarily go for the obvious things – the little things – but think seriously about your life in general and keep a diary of all the big things that you feel might be preying on your mind but which you may be carefully avoiding thinking about. See if you can deal with some of these bigger things but don't 'bite off' too much at one time. Just take one thing at a time, think carefully about how you can decrease the pressure on you from that one thing, and if that works OK, then go on to the next.

● TAKING IT OUT ON FRIENDS AND FAMILY

Dear Ann, **I get really stressed easily and I take it out on my friends and boys or smoke. What shall I do to not let everything get to me?** Girl aged 13.

Dear 'Take it out on friends, boys or smoking' – You could say that's what friends are for. If they are good friends, they will listen to you downloading your stress onto them and help support you. Boys can be friends just as much as girls, so they can do the same thing. But just remember, when they are stressed and want to download onto you, you have to listen to them just as they listened to you. Many people think that smoking helps to decrease their stress, and a huge number of cigarettes must get smoked for this reason alone. But your poor lungs and your poor body might well be feeling some stress themselves from having all those cancer substances forced on them! I can quite understand you not being able to quit smoking while you are still stressed, so you are going to have to find ways of dealing with your stress first – by talking to people about it, taking exercise, or doing some of the things suggested by young people in chapter 9. Then you need to think how you can best quit smoking.

Dear Doctor Ann, **Is it O.K. to punch your sister when you're stressed.** 14 year old girl.

 *Dear 'Is it OK to punch your sister when you're stressed'* – No, it is not all right. You will just stress your sister, who will then hit you back and increase your stress levels even more! If you think it will help, do find something to hit that won't get hurt and that won't hurt you. That doesn't mean getting at your cat, but your duvet or even your mattress might do.

● SMOKING FAGS

Dear Doctor Ann, **My mum doesn't like me smoking but I'm addicted 'cos I'm in stress. I smoke behind my mum's back. She caught me a while back and keeps me in the house. Plz help me. I don't want to lose my mum plz!!!** Girl aged 14.

Dear 'Smoke 'cos I'm stressed' – I have total sympathy with both you and your mum. The first thing I would like to do is to make all the top people in tobacco manufacturing smoke around 100 of their own cigarettes every day. This would greatly increase their stress, as they are well aware of the health effects and deaths caused by their products, and it

might, in the long run, greatly decrease my stress over having to see huge numbers of patients dying from smoking their products. It might finally persuade the manufacturers to stop producing their killer cigarettes. But your problem is more immediate than this. You need to approach your problem in two ways. The first is to ask yourself what is causing you stress and try to deal with that. The second is to quit smoking as a way of dealing with your stress. But you may not succeed with the second unless you first deal with the first. I would suggest that you start by talking to your mum about why you are stressed and asking her advice on how to deal with it. Then you can ask your mum if she can go to the doctor's with you to get more advice and maybe nicotine patches to help you stop smoking. Your mum, I am sure, would want to help you in any way she can.

Dear Doctor Ann, **Why do I get stressed, and why do I turn to fags and food? Please write back and help me to quit.** Girl aged 14.

Dear 'Stressed and turning to fags and food' – I think you and half the rest of the stressed people in the western world turn to fags and food. It is possibly the most common way that people try to cope with the pressures of everyday life, and of course smoking and overeating can lead to further pressures themselves. But let's face it, half the stressed world would not turn to fags and food if it did not at least give them the impression of helping – so you have my sympathy, if not my approval. There are better ways of dealing with stress, and many of them, recommended by young people themselves, are outlined in chapter 9. They include listening to music, taking time out, exercising, talking to other people about the things that stress you, and writing down the things that cause you stress. By the way, I wouldn't try to give up smoking and eating too much at the same time. Try quitting smoking first and see how you get on, then cut down on the amount of food. If you have gained a bit too much weight from all that eating, exercising will help you lose weight and help your stress.

Need to find out more?

Teenage Health Freak

The Diary of a Teenage Health Freak (3rd edition, OUP 2002) The book that got it all going. Read the latest version of Pete Payne's celebrated diary in all its gory detail, to find out pretty much all you need to know about your health, your body and how it works (or doesn't – whatever).

The Diary of the Other Health Freak (3rd edition, OUP 2002) The book that kept it all going. Pete's sister Susie sets out to outshine her big brother with a diary of her own, bringing the feminine touch to a huge range of teenage issues – sex, drugs, relationships, the lot.

Teenage Health Freak websites

www.teenagehealthfreak.org
www.doctorann.org
Two linked websites for young people. Catch up on the daily diary of Pete Payne, age 15 – still plagued by zits, a dodgy sex life, a pestilent sister... Jump to Doctor Ann's virtual surgery for all you want to know about fatness and farting, sex and stress, drinking and drugs, pimples and periods, hormones and headaches, and a million other things.

Other websites for teenagers

BBC kids' health
www.bbc.co.uk/health/kids

Mind Body Soul
www.mindbodysoul.gov.uk

Lifebytes
www.lifebytes.gov.uk

NSF young people's project site
www.at-ease.nsf.org.uk

There4me
www.there4me.com

All these sites give lots of information about health, sex and relationships.

Stressed, depressed, down or suicidal

ChildLine
Royal Mail Building,
Studd Street, London NW1 0QW
Freepost 1111, London N1 0BR
Tel: 020 7239 1000
Helpline: 0800 1111 (24 hours a day, every day of the year)
www.childline.org.uk
Provides a national telephone helpline for children and young people in danger or distress, who want to talk to a trained counsellor. All calls are free and confidential.

The Samaritans

Helpline: 08457 909090
www.samaritans.org.uk
Someone will always listen to you and your problems any time of the day or night, and it costs nothing for the call.

Alcohol
Drinkline

Helpline: 0800 917 8282
(9 am–11 pm, Mon–Fri;
6 pm–11 pm, Sat–Sun)
National Alcohol Helpline – provides telephone advice, leaflets and information about local groups.

Bereavement
RD4U

Free helpline: 0808 808 1677
(9.30 am–5 pm, Mon–Fri)
www.RD4U.org.uk
RD4U is part of CRUSE Bereavement Care's Youth involvement project. It exists to support people after the death of someone close.

Bullying
Anti-Bullying Campaign

185 Tower Bridge Road, London
SE1 2UF
Tel: 020 7378 1446
Gives telephone advice for young people who are being bullied. There are also some websites where you can get help...

Bullying Online

www.bullying.co.uk

Pupilline

www.pupilline.com

Eating disorders
Eating Disorders Association (EDA)

First Floor, Wensume House,
103 Prince of Wales Road,
Norwich NR1 1DW
Youth helpline: 01603 765050
(4–6 pm Mon–Fri)
www.edauk.com
Youth helpline for those aged 18 years and younger. Aims to help and support all those affected by anorexia and bulimia, especially sufferers, the families of sufferers and other carers.

If you are ill
NHS Direct

Tel: 0845 4647
www.nhsdirect.nhs.uk
Talk to a nurse on the phone about any health problem you are worried about.

National Aids Helpline

Tel: 0800 567123
(free and confidential; available 24 hours a day, 7 days a week)
Questions or worries about Aids can be discussed with a trained adviser.

Sex and everything attached

www.Ruthinking.co.uk
A great website about sex, relationships and all that stuff.

Brook Advisory Service
Young people's helpline:
0800 0185 023
www.brook.org.uk
User-friendly information service, offering advice on sex and contraception for all young people. Will tell you all about local clinics and send you leaflets even if you are under 16.

fpa (formerly The Family Planning Association)
2–12 Pentonville Road,
London N1 9FP
Tel: 020 7837 5432
Helpline: 0845 310 1334
(9 am–7 pm, Mon–Fri)
Gives information on all aspects of contraception and sexual health. Free fun leaflets available. They also run a telephone helpline for anyone who wants information on contraception and sexual health. Phone the helpline number to find the nearest fpa clinic in your area.

BAAF (British Agencies for Adoption and Fostering)
Tel: 020 7593 2000
(9 am–5 pm, Mon–Fri)
www.baaf.org.uk

A central agency for organizations involved in adoption and fostering. Publishes useful information leaflets and books about various aspects of adoption. Offers advice on tracing.

Rape Crisis Helplines
Look in the telephone directory or ring Directory Enquiries on 192 for the Helpline number in your area. Provides free confidential support and advice to victims of rape.

Lesbian and Gay Switchboard
Tel: 020 7837 7324
(24 hours a day)
www.llgs.org.uk
(this is the London and national Switchboard; there are also a number of regional Switchboards) Offers information and advice to lesbians and gay men and their families and friends.

Smoking
QUIT
Quitline: 0800 002200
(1 pm–9 pm)
www.quit.org.uk
Want to give up smoking? Phone this line for help.

Index